D1068863

# Animal Welfare 101

How to Raise Unique Pets Such as Amphibians, Cats, Dogs, Fish, Reptiles, and More From A to Z

## HowExpert with Jessica Child

## Copyright HowExpert™
### www.HowExpert.com

**For more tips related to this topic, visit www.HowExpert.com/animalwelfare.**

# Recommended Resources

[www.HowExpert.com](www.HowExpert.com) – Quick 'How To' Guides on Unique Topics by Everyday Experts.

[www.HowExpert.com/writers](www.HowExpert.com/writers) - Write About Your #1 Passion/Knowledge/Experience.

[www.HowExpert.com/membership](www.HowExpert.com/membership) - Learn a New 'How To' Topic About Practically Everything Every Week.

[www.HowExpert.com/jobs](www.HowExpert.com/jobs) - Check Out HowExpert Jobs.

# Table of Contents

# Animal Welfare Introduction

This book is dedicated to the animal and creature lover who sees an animal and wants to see it thrive in their home but hasn't yet made heads or tails of vague care sheets and conflicting information.

This eBook isn't an ultimate guide on how to care for each, individual pet since each species has a breadth of its own needs and preferences. Even further, every pet and its care changes constantly as we grow and change.

There will always be a new book, article, and expert that tells you what is out and what is in, but the core needs of your pet will never change (even as we better understand what those needs are).

Fish are a major example, as aquatic habitats have gone from colored gravel with plastic plants to carefully crafted underwater scenes with meticulously selected fish and complementing plants. However, shrimp have and always will love algae and having a safe, comfortable place to hide. We also now realize they thrive better with a variety of minerals in the water as well.

Instead of being a complete guide, this book aims to teach you how to think about what you want to keep and how to keep it. In each category, we will cover what type of pet you might consider and how to decide if it is something you would enjoy having.

We will consider the natural habitat of these pets and how to replicate them, what types of species will live this habitat, and what foods are best and most nutritious for them. Our goal is to provide them everything they need on a regular basis, so they can live as long as possible!

As you delve deeper into caring for your pets, keep in mind that the Animal Welfare hobby is large, as generic as it is specific, and filled with others who want to share their knowledge. There is always a forum or store filled with people who want to answer your questions, maximize the health of your friends, and get you further hooked!

My first piece of advice as an enthusiast is to find a local resource. If you keep cats or dogs, a good vet is your priority. If you can find a vet who works with other types of pets, that's definitely a good idea. For aquatics, reptiles, etc. it is good to find a quality local pet store that is run by enthusiasts. You're looking for someone who makes a living on their expertise with your pet's care, not just selling you something. They will be who you can call in an emergency just as much as somebody you can pass a question by.

# Chapter 1: Above Ground, Underwater: Amphibian Husbandry

When you're considering an amphibian, you're considering a group of animals that live anywhere a reliable body of water exists. When referring to amphibians, we usually mean vertebrates belonging t the class amphibia. We mean creatures like frogs and salamanders with slick skin that can breathe and wal outside of water even long term. They are cold blooded and can breathe through their skin. In adulthood, they may never need to swim in water again (and may be legitimately terrible at it), but they will still need a humid environment to thrive.

At the same time, amphibious is a term that implies the ability to survive on land as well as water. This makes this conversation more complicated simply because amphibious is a term that can be applied to invertebrates and reptiles as well. Their care needs may resemble an amphibian's, but they still require attention to their true species' needs as well. An example is that aquatic and semi-aquatic turtles may have amphibious qualities, but they are still part of the reptile family and require lighting (such as UVA/B) that a tree frog wouldn't require.

# Habitat & Environment

You will find an amphibian in nearly any biome in the world. If there is water on a consistent basis, you will probably find amphibians.

This section should give you an idea of what habitats you can have and if it's a habitat you would want to maintain.

Among all of them, you'll find these common elements.

Amphibians have delicate skin and anything living within water is likely sensitive to chlorine. Use dechlorinated water wherever possible.

Avoid any soil with fertilizer in it. Look for organic soils without added chemicals.

Damp enclosures with lights are likely to grow algae. Wipe it down with a damp, plain paper towel without print or an aquarium algae scraper.

While reptiles may require basking spots and special lighting, most amphibians are happy to just have a consistent light schedule. This is easily achieved with aquarium lighting and a timer. I've found that LED hosts more benefits than just its low energy requirements. They're getting more attractive and cheaper all the time and are including more features such as a wind down lighting. A good light spectrum is also enough to keep live plants happy long term!

Timers come in a variety of options, even smart timers that connect to your phone and easily handle complicated schedules, but their best benefit is that they can provide consistency we may sometimes slip on. It's also one less thing to worry about.

As far as the habitat you keep, this goes back to replicating their natural environment! Whether they naturally come from the rainforest or a pond in the chilly mountains, they usually fall into just a few categories: Arboreal, terrestrial, aquatic, or somewhere in between.

If you decide to set up a naturalistic habitat, I have found Joshsfrogs and SerpaDesign have the most thorough instructions for how to do this!

## *Half & Half: A Paludarium*

Although most amphibians need humidity and a source of water, some are specialized around the ability to be in water as much as out of it. Salamanders, morphing tadpoles, and turtles would all require this type of set up. Most humidity loving creatures will love this set up as well! Just block off areas they could get stuck in and include extra ways out (carefully placed sticks, rocks, fake vines) for the less aquatically inclined.

With this habitat, your goal is to replicate the base of a waterfall or where land meets a body of water (rivers, lakes, ponds, etc.).

To achieve this, your enclosure will have a sizeable water portion with a significant amount of land as well. A paludarium can be made in any water tight enclosure from a standard aquarium tank to an ExoTerra style enclosure.

Maintenance on this enclosure includes water changes, filtering (if you can fit one in), and cleaning the enclosure down. Water changes for paludariums are better more frequent than not and should be 20-90%. If you keep fish in the paludarium, do 20% weekly and up to 75% for larger changes when the water seems dirty. If there are no fish, you can change nearly all the water.

Always remember to dechlorinate the water. Nearly any dechlorinator works fine, just follow the instructions.

As always with aquatic areas, the larger it is, the fewer, though larger, changes you should do.

You should also use a good soil in these set ups. Change every few weeks unless you have a naturalistic paludarium, in which case the soil should last for years and only need replacement once the soil quality has degraded and no longer smells like the forest.

If you choose a bio-active paludarium, you'll need a variety of aquatic and high moisture plants as well as isopods and springtails (who will benefit from a soil with a variety of decaying matter). These additions will act as a clean-up crew to break down most of the waste your pets produce!

You'll still want to do water changes, though, and happy plants will require consistent trimming.

If any area starts to dry out, you'll want to spritz it. A misting system could be helpful if this is frequent and severe or generally forgotten.


## *Down to Earth: Terrestrial*

The benefit to this type of enclosure is there's no filtering or water changes! A fully terrestrial enclosure most benefits, well, terrestrial inhabitants. Common terrestrial amphibians are terrestrial salamanders and frogs (including dart frogs).

You'll simply make a moist soil for your pet, usually based on coco fiber and sphagnum moss. Your pet usually requires a water bowl, and possibly a hut.

The water bowl should be cleaned and refilled any time it's soiled (with some ornery pets, this might be daily or more), and the soil will need to be spot cleaned daily and replaced about every two weeks. You can use wet paper towels short term, but it won't feel very natural or comfortable for your pet long term and could end up stressing them out.

If you have a burrowing pet, such as a pixie frog, you'll need to keep two things in mind. The soil should be high enough for the frog to burrow completely, which could be a lot as your frog grows. You should also plan on not having a bio active enclosure. Even if your frog doesn't eat your isopods, it might uproot your plants nd the soil replacements could be hard on your lants.

ou could, however, keep plants in a pot or even use a errarium making method to make the back and sides lore attractive.

f you are keeping dart frogs, you can make a mostly ioactive terrarium, with plants and tree bark and loss wherever. You'll want to litter the ground with eaves for the frogs to hide under as well. Expect your ttle dart frogs to potentially eat spring tails and ossibly small isopods. These tiny hunters love tiny nsects!

## oo% Humidity: Aquatic

ome amphibians don't ever emerge from the water. Vhile they resemble their more adaptable ounterparts, they won't survive on land, or at least, or long. We will mostly see aquatic salamanders, rogs, and turtles. For these pets, they will need an mple aquatic option regardless of your enclosure hoice.

)verall, they need care very much like fish.

hoose an enclosure you can fill with enough water to un a filter. With the water being their primary home, quatic species will need clean water to breathe and ive in. In an ideal world, dechlorinated and clean vater is all your pet wants. Unfortunately, the reality s more complicated.

Not all aquatic amphibians will need a substrate and may do without, but this is another area where naturalistic can help. Live plants can help filter additional waste, produce oxygen for the water, and compete with algae. However, some water inhabitant love to munch on plants! Make sure your pet isn't inclined eat them before you invest in plants.

Choose a soil or gravel that best meets your pet's needs (e.g. if it prefers gravel, choose gravel). You should be able to find many plants that complement this substrate. In my experience, anything living in water will see a quality of life improvement with plants (as long as they don't eat them all down). Bore and sluggish pets can come to life! They love to run between plants, and they feel much more secure with hiding places.

You can also add hiding places in the form of driftwood or aquarium decorations. Make sure any hiding places have more than ample room for your pe to get in and out, even when they grow. A sudden growth spurt could cause substantial injuries trying to get in and out of their hiding places.

Determine the difference between your home's temperature year-round and your pet's needs. I've found it's common to need to run a cooler for an axolotl, who prefer temperatures below 75F (24C), and closer to 60-64F (16-18C). Some people also accomplish this with tricks like frozen water bottles. Otherwise, some species might like to be at 75F (24C) and that might mean a heater for those in climates with a winter.

After that, it's just maintenance!

Algae outbreaks are the bane of any aquarist's life, so account for this in your aquarium care! You will need to do water changes and remove any algae outbreaks taking over. Algae isn't just ugly, it can choke out your live plants, create poor conditions for your pets to survive, and even harbor harmful bacteria cultures. If you have severe or frequent algae outbreaks, the simple answer is that you have enough nutrients in your water for it to thrive.

Algae nutrients include chemicals added for our live plants, excess waste, and lighting. If you have frequent algae outbreaks, reducing your light cycle and introducing a 2 hour break during the light cycle can reduce it. You'll also want to reduce the dosage of any aquatic plant fertilizers and increase water changes.

All of that said, the complicated but short answer is... you'll always be fighting algae. No aquarist gets away with this one.

Aquatic set ups also need frequent water changes, at least 20-25% a week. Make them more frequent if fighting algae or things just don't seem right. Water changes are almost always the first troubleshooting step in aquarium care.

You can remove more than 20-25% in a water change, but only up to 75% or so. Beneficial bacteria in the water and on the ceramic stones of the filter (never wash these!) help break down harmful substances in your water. If you replace too much water, you can harm these colonies and make the water difficult to inhabit.

Aquatic care will be covered more in depth in Chapter 2: Aquatic Husbandry.


## _Up Above and Far Away: Arboreal_

An arboreal set up is particular to pets that like to climb trees and anything else they can in order to be far above the ground. As far as amphibians go, you're usually considering a tree frog. Tree frogs come in a huge variety and live in forests throughout the world. In general, all they're asking for is one thing: Something to climb.

You can technically put anything safe for your pet to touch on the bottom of an arboreal set up. While you don't want larger pieces, the frog could swallow as a substrate, they don't really care whether it's paper towels or a plush soil bed.

I tend to find tree frogs are hilariously clumsy and are resilient to a few tumbles, but it's an important thought to keep in mind.

Expect them to fall.

They'll appreciate something soft to stumble onto. They'll also appreciate not having to dodge anything sharp, pointed, or especially hard on the ground, such as rocks, gravel, or pointed plants.

They want things to climb. Our frogs climb trees (fake or real), fake vines, sticks, and walls. They also love to crawl on wall-mounted plants and, geez, our misting ystem. Expect them to flip any unsecured plants and ilt any outlets for a misting system. These mischievous spirits will explore every nook and cranny of a terrarium and try to make a mess of it.

Despite their goals to reach for the stars, they are still amphibians and need moisture. This is another positive for a paludarium or base with substrate. Anything that helps hold moisture will benefit your frogs. If you have good air movement, you'll likely need to spritz or mist the enclosure. It's another setting where a misting system can simplify your life.

Maintenance is spot cleaning and washing down anything that looks iffy. Replace any substrate over time as it gets gross, though tree frogs will make their messes higher up than a terrestrial species.

If you choose to go bioactive in an arboreal set up, there won't be too much maintenance. Your plants and clean-up crew of isopods and springtails can do most of your work. You will need to trim plants and clean algae build up off the sides (a good reason most of these enclosures are glass). A drainage layer (you can use clay balls or specialized drainage materials) will keep your soil from getting water logged and rotting. You'll also want to occasionally replace the soil once it looks more like mud than soil as the plants and invertebrates work through it. However, this timeline is more of a year or more (depending on the depth and use) than a couple of weeks.

# Types of Amphibians

Amphibians and amphibious species cover a wide array of environments and needs. You'll find a few that frequently pop up whether due to their ease of care, stunning nature, or their proclivity to breed in captivity. For easy, common, and captive bred, you'll find the list commonly narrows to salamanders and frogs.

## _Terrestrial and Aquatic Salamanders_

Salamanders are true amphibians, born as larvae that eventually grow legs and form the rest of their bodies. Most salamanders you'll find are aquatic, terrestrial, or somewhere between. Few are arboreal, and rarely found in the pet trade. Here are three common options!

Fire Salamanders are burrowing salamanders and the first salamander to be taxonomically described! These beautiful salamanders will survive in terrestrial and paludarium set ups. They are enthusiastic carnivores normally fed insects and earthworms and may occasionally eat a small enough frog or fish. They get to around 6-12" (15-35 cm) and live an average of 6-12 years.

Marbled Salamanders are also burrowing salamanders. These goofy-faced pets will benefit best from a terrestrial enclosure that allows them to burrow. They are carnivorous and will eat insects, orms, slugs, and snails. They will reach 3"-5" (7-3cm) in size and live about four years.

xolotls are an aquatic salamander, popular for their eautiful external gills that they keep throughout their ves. They live their full lives in water, so an aquatic nclosure or a paludarium with a sizeable water ortion of 15-20 gallon (55-80 liters) would be a good t. These carnivores eat a huge variety of foods in the ild and captivity! Not only insectivores, they can eat nails, worms, crustaceans, small fish and mphibians, a variety of worms, brine shrimp, and sh pellets. These salamanders should be kept alone. hese silly salamanders get up to 10" (25 cm) in size nd can live a happy 15 years!

## rogs

rogs encompass a massive spectrum of options, even vhen we narrow our options down to pets that are asy to keep! These goofballs live everywhere in the vorld and wild and can bring a smile to nearly any pet eeper's face. Here are three very easy frogs for a eginner.

)umpy tree frogs are common, inexpensive, and a requent beginner frog for a reason: They're easy. hey're hardy, mild mannered, and voracious eaters. )o expect them to mistake you for food, but they do ιot have teeth. These active arboreal frogs will thrive n an arboreal set up with lots to explore. They also ιeed a well secured habitat as they tend to open any ιnsecured pieces. They are carnivores who will eat

21

insects, small fish and frogs, pinky mice, and, maybe, your fingers. They will reach around 4" (10cm) and live up to 16 years.

Pac-Man frogs, or South American Horned frogs, are more and more common these days and known for their round shape and large mouth that resemble Pac Man. These fun frogs are being bred into a variety of color morphs to choose from. Adults will need enclosures the size of a 10 to 20-gallon tank where they can burrow. Unlike Pac-Man, they find that they can sit-and-wait for food to show up, so expect them to be low activity. These carnivores will eat anything that passes by and will fit in their mouths. Their recommended diet is crickets, dubia roaches, and nightcrawlers. These enthusiastic eaters should be kept alone.

Pixie frogs, or the African bullfrog, are nicknamed after their genus, and certainly not after their size. An exception to the amphibian rule, females are usually smaller than males by about half the size. When it comes to males, these giants can easily inch toward 5 pounds (over 2kg) with some reaching over 9 inches (23cm). A minimum of a 20-gallon sized tank is needed, while a 24x18x18 inch Exo Terra (or similar style) enclosure is recommended. They are sit-and-wait and you'll find they aren't very active. These carnivores eat almost anything on the menu including crickets, Dubia roaches, hornworms, nightcrawlers, mice (frozen or thawed), black solider fly larvae, superworms, butterworms, or nearly any feeder insec you can find that will fit in its mouth. These frogs should certainly be kept alone.

## Dart Frogs

You might notice dart frogs and their tadpoles being sold in many stores recently. These are not beginner frogs, nor are they poisonous in captivity (they produce poisons from foods not eaten in captivity). They have special humidity and habitat requirements including an abundance of hiding options with a carpet of leaf litter to hide beneath. They also feed from very small insects such as springtails, isopods, and fruit flies. As tempting and gorgeous as these pets are, it is best to get your feet wet before tackling this enchanting creature!

# Your Hungry Amphibian

You'll find most guides are clear for what to feed your amphibian and what to do. They may also be a little vague at times. I've found this has to do with simply learning the habits of your pet, like coming out to hunt for food or settling into their favorite hiding spot even at feeding time.

My first frogs, Dumpy Tree Frogs, had me scouring the internet demanding to know exactly how many crickets, at what size, should be fed, and how often. It turned out that these frogs are looking for a balance between having a flab of skin next to their ear and that flab never covering their ears. I found their balance was perfect with varied feedings every other day.

With obesity prone species, it's important to learn what obesity looks like in that species and learn your pet's habits to keep them below that point. Otherwise in many species, they are better at self-regulating and you can determine their needs based on what is leftover after a set amount of time (e.g. for dart frogs, what's left at next feeding).

Overall, learning what exactly to feed your pet comes from selecting options from the general list of what your pet will accept and trying them out. Your pet is an individual and will usually express preferences and opinions.

Let's look at what you might be feeding your amphibians and what they like to eat!

We'll cover these all again, more in depth, in Chapter 7: Slithering, Pattering Reptiles.

## *Insects and worms*

Your amphibians will benefit from a variety of crickets, black soldier fly and their larvae, fruit flies, and dubia roaches for their day-to-day eating. They can accept wax worms and hornworms as special high-fat treats. You may also feed mealworms and the less chitinous superworms, but some keepers feel these are still too much for an amphibian's belly.

Another option is nightcrawlers and earthworms. Do not collect these in the wild as they may have been exposed to chemicals that can make your pet sick. Do purchase them from a source that understands the importance of the worms being clean and free of chemicals. These are a great high protein source for some amphibians!

Choose flightless fruit flies, pinhead crickets, and black soldier flies for smaller pets, depending on their preference.

For the rest, choose what they will readily eat and what your pet is large enough to eat. Rotate through them from there.

## *Pinky mice*

Some people like to feed their amphibians this high fat treat! This is best reserved for very large frogs that can swallow the mouse. They should be frozen or thawed and not live. Some keepers would recommend against ever using a pinky mouse due to their significant amount of fat and bones. Ultimately, this is up to the individual. Just consider if your amphibian truly is large enough to handle this size of a treat.

## *Cannibalism*

This one is strongly recommended against, of course. However, it's an important consideration. Some frogs especially have a strong tendency to eat other frogs they can fit in their mouths. Before you bring an amphibian home, consider whether it is likely to eat any of your other pets or if you should be bringing home more than one.

In the case of white's tree frogs, they are both able to be housed with others of the same species *and* very likely to eat any frog they can fit into their mouths, so never buy one smaller than what you have. These are also very clever frogs that like to get out, so make sure they are well secured and won't wander into any other enclosures.

## ***Supplements***

Amphibians benefit from a rotation of calcium with Vitamin D3 and calcium without Vitamin D3. When considering vitamins, amphibians can't accept the safer beta carotene as a source of Vitamin A and may need retinol which is easier to overdose on.

The recommended rotation for supplements is twice a week with calcium, one each with and without D3, and once a week with vitamins.

# Review of Amphibians

Amphibians are truly a fantastic first choice for getting into amphibian and reptile husbandry.

Choosing an amphibian is as simple as deciding what kind of habitat you can keep, whether it's short or tall, and whether you would be willing to do a water change.

Once you know what type of enclosure and amphibian you want, also consider what kind of food you'd like to keep on hand and what you can get ahold of. It's a good idea to have your supplements and foods secured prior to bringing your amphibian home. The best part of the easy choices such as the listed frogs and salamanders is that they eat common, easy to care for foods.

If you choose more complicated foods like fruit flies, keep in mind they do have some additional care needs.

Once you have these things decided, simply enjoy your new friend and their individual habits!

# Chapter 2: Bubbles and Splashes: Aquatic Husbandry

Anywhere there's naturally occurring water, there's usually aquatic creatures. In this chapter, we'll cover what common habitats are kept, what to keep, and what to feed it.

Something to know before you start is that aquatic care can be very complicated and chemistry heavy. If you've experienced failures with keeping fish before, you'll find more and more that it's not as simple as it seems at the surface.

Maintaining your water quality involves a lot of different factors. Many fish have different personalities and growth expectations than unscrupulous fish sellers will tell you. Fish that are sick in a tank with invertebrates like snails can cause conundrums. Not all products are created equal and can be costly mistakes or simply a waste of your money and effort. These are all common problems fish keepers encounter.

Regardless, fish keepers often find it's worth the growing pains!

This hobby is much easier to keep up with if you find a reputable fish store nearby. A local fish store/shop (LFS) can provide more resources than just saving on shipping. A good local fish shop will become a resource for all your questions and needs and can often order specific types of fish or products you may need. These shops are marked by sincere and honest

taff who are happy to let you know that a common
pleco will be too big for any indoor aquarium, won't
sell you sick fish, and keep clean tanks with happy,
not dead, fish. These stores are invaluable resources
for beginners and experts alike and are well worth
some additional driving over low-quality shops.

# Aquatic Habitats

There are a few main habitats you'll encounter, but
since water occurs naturally in so many
environments, any of these will seem generic once you
become acquainted to your pet's needs. Even the
reliable occurrence of ponds and puddles of every
variety and size creates special requirements for a fish
to thrive in. Once you have a good idea of what you
want and what these groups look like, adjusting your
parameters becomes a breeze!

## _Freshwater_

This is the most common and easiest way to start!
However, don't underestimate it as a beginner step.
Many people find that freshwater is challenging and
intriguing enough to keep them occupied and fill their
home with pets they love.

One option is the basic setup that many stores offer
options for. A cheap gravel and plastic plants. It will
work, and you can have happy, healthy fish. However,
plastic plants wear down and don't do anything to

fight off algae. Some types of fake plants can even become so inundated with algae that they cannot be cleaned.

You can keep a naturalistic setup with live plants that help break down ammonia and other harmful compounds as well as add oxygen. This production is significant enough that some very well-tuned tanks, usually using CO2 injections, have plants that produc so much oxygen that they release oxygen bubbles from their leaves. Plants will need additional fertilizers, soil or gravel consideration, and for some plants, CO2. CO2 comes either in a tank with a diffuser or in chemical form poured from a bottle. There's plenty of debate within the community about which is better, especially with DIY options for both, so your mileage may vary.

You can also try aquascaping, a hobby within the hobby, of creating picturesque and artful displays of plants and hard materials such as dragon stone, seiry stone, volcanic rock, and highly nutritious soil. Do keep in mind these aquariums do have a steeper set up price since they are meant to be art and top of the line.

I've also seen a lot of fish stores selling small aquascaped tanks that are cycled and stocked with fish if you'd rather not deal with the set up. Examine the contents and included equipment to see if this is a good deal. If they want a new display, they may drop the price below the cost of the equipment and fish separately. Not only that, they can give you any advice on keeping everything healthy like they have!

One important choice no matter what type of freshwater tank you decide to keep is the lighting. Sometimes, saltwater lighting is more attractive, cheaper, or has nicer features. However, saltwater lighting includes a blue spectrum of light. If you cannot turn this off, do not use it for a freshwater aquarium or it will encourage algae growth since freshwater plants do not need this spectrum.

As far as what parameters to keep your water at, decide on what fish you want next! The size of your tank, the temperature, and the minerals of the water are all dependent of what will live in it. What you can keep in a freshwater tank is a massive and exciting list that changes constantly, from miniature fish to gigantic discus to bubbly pufferfish to even small sharks and rays!

## _Freshwater and general tank maintenance_

Maintenance for a freshwater tank is a little more complicated than filling a container with water.

First, any fish tank is best off with good filtration. Good filtration reduces the buildup of nitrogen compounds as well as ammonia while adding oxygen for your fish to breathe.

Canister filters are fantastic options that pull the water out of the tank to a a separate canister with layers of carbon, sponges, and ceramic. Carbon should be replaced regularly, while sponges can be rinsed off in fish water. Ceramic should never be rinsed since it houses beneficial bacteria.

Sump tanks are tanks with three sections. One section for the inflow of water, another section for filtration options (these vary based on your tank and what type of water you have), and a third for pumping water and sometimes adding oxygen flow. Since these can be a little more complicated, beginners usually do best with a canister or the familiar hang-on-back filter.

In many homes, a heater will be necessary. As far as which one to buy, you will get what you pay for. Cheap ones tend to break in one way or another, such as never turning off or never turning on, or worse, being poorly designed and becoming fire hazards. However, know that any thermometer brand has defects and failures, you'll just find that some brands have fewer than others. As a result, any time you check on your fish, check their temperature.

Some thermometers have displays for what temperature the tank is, but those are also fallible. Keep a reliable thermometer, such as a waterproof probe instant read thermometer handy. These are generally very cheap and accurate and can read in about 3 seconds.

Of course, all water should be dechlorinated. This can be done with or without a stress coat, and generally, any method of dechlorination will work well. Don't fret over the brand you use; most any will do. With chemical dechlorination, one thing to note is that stress coat can be overdosed while a non-stress coat product would require a considerable amount to verdose. Also, regular dechlorinator can be urchased by the gallon for cheap.

Text, you'll want to consider the quality of your water ource. Some fish prefer hard water or soft water. This an be an easy adjustment depending on what your ource is. A simple water test can tell you if your water hard or soft, but a quick question is, does you water ave soap scum in your tub and residue on your lasses? If yes, it's probably hard. A TDS meter or ardness test kit can give you specifics, but some LFS an help you with testing and recommendations.

hose with serious concerns about their water or hose who need to do a lot of work to make their water ight for their fish usually resort to a reverse osmosis ystem. These systems are a little pricier, but they trip the water of nearly any minerals as well as hlorine. For some fish, the right balance of minerals ill need to be added back in. This is a significant elief in money and time for some keepers.

Once you set up your fish tank, you'll let it run for a while without any fish of any kind in it. Some people dd a few drops of pure ammonia per gallon/liter or ome fish flakes to jump start the ammonia cycle. Older advice is to add a cheap fish, but this will likely ill the fish and seems a bit cruel.

You should have an API master test kit on hand for esting. If you find the caps don't seal well and dribble r pulling water from your tank is frustrating, I've ound replacing their test tubes with my own and using clean syringes to pull water is easier and nvolves less spilling than their included kit.

Regardless, their tubes work just fine, so this isn't a priority.

Test your new aquarium frequently while it goes through the nitrogen cycle. This could take up to 45 days.

With added ammonia, you'll see ammonia test very high at first. In time, the bacteria colonies will grow i your soil and filter and begin to break it down into nitrites and, finally, nitrates. Your water isn't yet inhabitable until the bacterial colonies are strong enough to break down the nitrites completely into nitrates. Essentially, watch for your nitrites to plummet and your nitrates to jump.

These bacteria are essential to keeping the quality of your water habitable, so take care of them! Do not wash your filter's ceramic pieces where many of them live, since this process can kill them. Carefully read al instructions on any chemicals you add since some are toxic to your bacteria. They can live indefinitely in your water and will adjust to your fish's load (but you'll still need water changes).

Every time you add a new fish to your aquarium, expect a jump in ammonia and nitrites as your bacterial colonies adjust, so keep an eye on the parameters and do additional water changes until things even back out. You'll also want to quarantine any new fish being added to an established tank. Another upside to a good LFS is that you'll rarely have an issue crop up in quarantine through them.

Once your tank is established, you'll need to do weekly water changes of 20-25%, and you'll only need to do more if your parameters are off or an illness or algae outbreak necessitates it. A rule of thumb is that larger tanks won't need as many water changes since they absorb little changes more easily.

Water changes even a degree from your current tank's temperature can stress your fish. The new water will likely be a little different, but you can minimize this with a thermometer. This is an area where the faster reading and highly accurate thermometers are indispensable.

No matter what type of aquarium you keep, algae is a lifetime battle. Spores cannot be killed because they are in air and bleaching your plants to avoid it usually only kills snail eggs, if it does that. If you have an algae outbreak, readjust your water changing and fertilizing habits as well as your lighting schedule. An algae outbreak signifies one thing: An abundance of nutrients the inhabitants aren't using. If you are not dealing with cyanobacteria, some keepers have had success with introducing a 2 hour "off" period during their day. This break is enough to slow down algae production without putting the plants to sleep. Cyanobacteria, however, is defeated only with sheer perseverance.

## Brackish

Brackish is water that's not quite salt water and not quite freshwater. In nature, these are usually areas where oceans meet rivers or other freshwater habitats. Its needs reflect this. You'll need to add marine salt to these tanks, generally use sand for the substrate, and check potential plants to ensure they can handle higher salinity.

Brackish tanks will require a hygrometer to ensure they aren't going above or below the ideal specific gravity of 1.005 to 1.020. You can do water changes to adjust this number. Make sure to mix your salt water outside of the tank and add it slowly.

Live plants that can handle brackish water will need to be acclimated slowly.

Other than that, brackish care is very similar to freshwater!

## _Saltwater_

Saltwater is a whole different bag of water.

In addition to freshwater parameters, saltwater needs to be monitored for salinity, alkalinity, calcium, and phosphates. These will require additional care to adjust as they rise and fall, as well as planning for what the inhabitants will require.

In general, I would strongly recommend against starting with a saltwater tank, at least until you have a reliable resource for your questions as well as some experience maintaining an aquarium.

# Types of Aquatic Pets

Aquatic pets vary from very easy to extremely difficult. To minimize the challenges, I'll stick with freshwater. This list will include a couple more challenging pets in addition to the easier ones since they are very popular.

Once you know where you like to go for a fish store, find out their stocking schedule. Fish that were just shipped and relocated to their show tanks are stressed. If you wait a few days, these fish should have lower stress levels and be more likely to thrive once they're home.

## Angelfish

These are beautiful and enchanting semi-aggressive cichlids that may not always get along with each other or other fish. They may be alright and never pose an issue, or they may kill and uproot your plants.

On the other hand, they really are beautiful fish that draws in many beginners. It's not unusual to see someone still learning the ropes do well with these fish!

These fish love high quality flakes and frozen foods!

## Betta fish

These extremely hardy and beautiful puddle fish can live in tanks as small as cups. However, your betta fish will be much happier in a tank large enough to explore and support a heater (to about 75-80°F or 24-26.7°C) and a filter.

These carnivorous fish will eat fish flakes, freeze dried foods, blood worms, and brine shrimp.

These are extremely aggressive fish that will eventually attack tank mates, even if they initially do well.

## Goldfish

Goldfish are large growing fish that can dirty their tanks quickly. They are hardy fish that may do alright for their lifetime, but they will not be happy. They are not good beginner fish or candidates for the average small beginner tank.

## Killifish

Killifish are stunning but small community fish that come in a huge variety of shapes and options, have easy tropical care, and accept a variety of foods. These are a beautiful and uncommon start for a beginning fish keeper but do keep in mind that they are very

mall and can be the target of many larger or
ggressive fish.

## Neocaridina and caridina (small shrimp)

Neocaridina (e.g. the cherry shrimp) are becoming a
obby in and of themselves. They come in delightful
ets of colors and patterns and are a joy to watch
vorking around the clock to eat through algae and
ellets!

hey could be an OK place to start for fish, as long as
couple important things are accounted for. Their
emperature should stay around 75°F (25°C), and if it
ontinues to rise too far, the shrimp can grow faster
han their shells and pass on. General hardness, or
H, is very important for these shrimps as well. You
hould test the water they'll be kept in for gH and
djust it to the proper range of the type you're
eeping. This is extremely important for their overall
ealth and ability to breed.

hese shrimps are extremely small and edible, and
nany fish would love to make a cocktail of them.
here aren't a lot of tankmates they can have other
han herbivorous snails, so many shrimp keepers
imply set aside a tank just for shrimp.

)nce you have a happy colony of shrimp and their
vater parameters are right, they are prolific breeders
nd will fill a tank in no time.

Don't forget that these fish like to eat algae! You'll enjoy fewer algae problems in tanks with these fish!

When feeding pellets, feed high quality food free of copper; this is toxic to these shrimps.

## *Plecos & Ancistrus & Otos*

The common pleco is not a good fit for the common aquarium. These massive fishes are best reserved for very large tanks and ponds as they are very wide, very tall, and very long. If you are in love with their personalities and shapes, like most of us, look instead at the Ancistrus. These goofy fish come in a huge variety of patterns, colors, and features (such as the medusa and bushynose pleco) while staying small enough for most aquariums. Their diets vary based on the Ancistrus in question.

Otocinclus, on the other hand, is a pretty specific fish that generally has a very mild non-aggressive temperament that, even giant sized, won't outgrow many aquariums.

Otocinclus and some Ancistrus will eat algae, and because they stay smaller, they'll stay more active. Ensure that the type of Ancistrus you're looking at isn't a carnivore before you bring them home for this job!

# Pufferfish

These highly intelligent fish demand more care than other fish and are not always good beginner fish.

This fish has two ongoing challenges throughout its life.

First, nearly all of them need pristine water. They will not do well in a dirty tank.

Second, they have beaks that continuously grow. They must be fed something enticing and hard enough to wear down their beaks, such a shellfish or snails. Without this, their beaks can overgrow and keep them from eating, starving them out. If they do overgrow, they can be trimmed, but this is a difficult process.

It is important to accurately identify what kind of pufferfish you would like to keep and either order it or get it through your LFS. When we got our humpback puffer, we ordered it through a LFS who got a handful in. This gave us a chance to look over the stock and decide which ones we wanted. An unintended side effect of this is that the LFS gets a lot of pufferfish in, and their sellers aren't always honest or correct about what kind it is. A reliable LFS will pick up on this before the fish is in your tank!

Some pufferfish are extremely large, some are very tiny, some are very aggressive, some are almost communal. It's important to understand your desired puffer's nature before bringing it home.

A side note for pufferfish, nearly all are wild caught. These fish have been stressed and exposed to many diseases in the wild. Check with your LFS if they've treated for parasites. If not, be prepared to. Pufferfish likely come with internal and external parasites. Even if you treat for parasites immediately, watch your puffer carefully for the first few months for signs to appear.

Your pufferfish's diet is particular to the kind you get and could be anything from life fish or worms to frozen cubes from a LFS to oysters purchased from a grocery store. It also depends on your puffer's personal preferences.

You'll also want to keep an eye on the water conditions of the puffer you have in mind. These fish are found in saltwater, brackish, and freshwater, and some are even up for debate which they do best in. Once you decide what kind of water you'd like to keep, make sure your pufferfish will be happy in it!

## _Rainbows_

This is a gorgeous fish that usually gets more colorful as it grows. In general, these fish can be very aggressive or friendly depending on the fish itself. It's a good idea to observe them in the store to choose which ones you like. Try not to keep more than one male together, as they may not get along.

These are another easy, tropical fish that will accept flakes and frozen foods!

# Rays

Rays charm us as children and adults, and we would surely like to keep these fish in our homes!

However, these fish are large and need a significant amount of space to roam in. I'd recommend against these fish unless you can keep a tank a minimum of 4'x4' (1.2mx1.2m) just for the smallest species.

# Snails & Shrimp

Snails are fantastic for beginners and experienced keepers! Depending on the species, they usually eat a variety of algaes and decaying plant matter.

Some will only breed in brackish conditions (such as the nerite), and some can breed in freshwater and even take over (such as the pond snail, commonly seen as a pest, though some of your fish will be delighted to find this snack).

Do keep an eye on your general hardness to ensure their shells will stay healthy and not disintegrate over time.

Do not stress if your snail retracts into its shell and floats at the top or lies on the bottom of your tank. These inconsiderate tricksters like to take extended naps. As a rule of thumb, if the trap is completely closed, they're alive.

You can also remove it and do other tests if you're worried. If you think it really is dead, you'll want to remove it before it spoils your water. You can put it under a light to check for a heartbeat. In addition, a dead snail smells awful, which is part of why is soils your water so quickly.

Shrimp, like the Amano and ghost shrimps, are great at keeping away algae as part of their natural diet. Shrimp are fantastic workers that you'll almost always find working!

There are a couple of things to consider when bringing home one of these shrimps. Ghost shrimp can be aggressive, especially in large groups. Amano, even if they lay eggs, can't reproduce in freshwater and may even eat baby shrimp such as neocaridinas.

Nerite snails are a popular choice for algae control as well. These sweet-natured snails come in a variety of patterns and even with thorns and cannot reproduce in freshwater even though they will likely lay eggs all over your tank.

## *Tetras*

Tetras are now commonly found in a huge variety other than just neon tetras and come in sizes from miniature to medium. These classics truly are great beginner fish. These are hardy communal fish that are happy to eat foods as simple as flakes and are happy in generic tropical conditions! Remember to find a balance: They need to be in a group, but that group shouldn't overstock your aquarium.

# Feeding a Hungry Fish!

Since fish exist in nearly any area of the world, they eat a massive variety of foods. Here are just a few you'll commonly find! If you have a large carnivore, it can be fun going through to see what kind of foods they like the best.

Aquarium water can dirty very quickly from overfeeding. Check on your fish's food after about five minutes and remove any excess.

Fish only need to be fed once a day, if that. Some fish, especially kept alone or with their own type, may only eat every few days or so. Other fish may turn on their tank mates if you skip a day.

## *Flakes & pellets*

Not all flakes are made the same.

Look for well-reviewed, high quality foods that list high quality ingredients on their label. These will vary based on what you're feeding. For herbivores, you should see things like spirulina high on the list. For carnivores, you should see a mixture of fish high on the list. Great quality flakes and pellets don't always

45

cost a premium and can be purchased in bulk for a discount so they're worth the additional legwork.

Of course, fish have preferences. Even if your fish refused pellets or flakes before, they might go crazy for the right kind! This is a personal preference you will have to work out with your fish.

## *Frozen foods*

Frozen foods for fish include beef heart (which can cause fish to grow quickly), blood shrimp, mysis shrimp, krill, daphnia, rotifers, spirulina, even clams. For saltwater specifically, there's also foods like coral and algae.

Thanks to all the options in this area, your fish can have a lot of variety in their diet. As always, your fish may also just not even like frozen foods.

To feed your fish frozen food, thaw a portion in a container with distilled water. Pour it into the tank or use a syringe or baster to distribute it.

## *Live foods*

Live foods are exciting for some fish, and wild caught fish especially can be particular about this option.

ome hobbyists would urge against using feeder fish old for very cheap at a store since they can carry arasites, but it is an option.

ive feeders also include plain crawfish, culled eocaridinas, ghost shrimp, worms, or small fish you oped wouldn't fit into another fish's mouth but efinitely did (yikes, err on the side of caution next ime).

Vorms (earthworms and nightcrawlers) are ometimes preferred due to their high protein ontent, variety of sizes, low price and availability, nd squirmy habits. Do not collect worms from utside and ensure those that you purchase are not xposed to chemicals such as pesticides and fertilizers ince these can make your fish sick and spread into he water. Some fish stores and sporting stores sell hese types.

## Seafood

f you have a carnivore like a pufferfish, they are pecialized in breaking open shellfish and eating early anything meaty. You can add variety to their liet with a simple stop by your seafood department or eafood specialist. Clams, cockles, mussels, scallops, quid and unshelled shrimp can be purchased fresh or rozen. Fresh shellfish should be frozen at least 48 ours to kill parasites. It can also be a good idea to haw them in distilled water before feeding.

## _Veggies_

If you have herbivorous fish, you can add variety to
their diets with fresh vegetables!

Purchase organic vegetables, wash them well, and
blanch or steam them until they are cooked. The goal
is to reduce any chemicals on it, remove anything that
is on them, kill any parasites and bacteria, and make
them easier to eat.

You can feed your fish deseeded cucumber, greens
such as bok choy, lima beans, peas, zucchini, and
more. Just check before you feed it.

# Review of Aquatics

Fish are a challenging pet to keep that are often
misrepresented in unscrupulous shops. I think we've
all walked into a shop and been told that common
pleco will look great in that 10-gallon or 40-liter tank
on that-there shelf, and yep, the nitrogen cycle isn't a
big deal, but you may as well add a few hundred tetra
while you're at it.

The reality is, aquatics require patience and intent,
and often-times, your tank will be happier and more
peaceful with fewer fish in it.

The process for a happy aquarium is as follows:

1. Deciding the type of water to maintain
   (freshwater, brackish, saltwater)

2. Deciding the type of aquarium to maintain (is it natural? glow in the dark?)
3. Deciding the size of aquarium you want (either because of space in your home, your devotion to moving twenty buckets, or a type of fish you want)
4. Nitrogen cycle (This is a great time to have any live plants added!)
5. Adding your fish and ensuring they acclimate well
6. Enjoying your fish. Try a variety of foods and revel in the success of finding their favorites!

# Chapter 3: Meowing, Purring: Cat Husbandry

Cats have been in our lives for centuries. Archaeologists are constantly finding more proof of these companions throughout history! Many of us know basic care for a cat, so this chapter is more of an overview of what to expect if you haven't yet made the jump!

## Caring for a feline familiar

Care for cats is relatively simple. Unlike dogs, there aren't really "working breed" cats that need duties or extensive exercise (your mileage may vary), and as mammals, they're happy in most any environment we are.

The best part about cats is that they need minimal vacation care and many owners find an extended day out doesn't cause them harm.

Before you bring a cat home, look for a vet and price out any regular care your cat will need, such as annual checkups, dental cleanings, and vaccines. You'll want to have a good handle on budgeting out the cost of food as well as regular and emergency vet visits. Your vet will also be your resource in case anything concerning ever happens or you just have questions.

# ood & Water

our cat, like any pet (especially fish), should always
ave access to water unless directed by a vet. This
uld be an auto release jug, and some people let their
ats share with the dog, that leaking faucet, or a bowl.
Iake sure to keep these clean to avoid a buildup of
nything icky. Also, fix that faucet.

s for food, the frequency and type comes down to a
onversation with your vet. In general, look for foods
1at are high in animal and fish derived proteins,
ather than proteins from plants. Since cats truly are
arnivores, they won't get much nutrition from plant-
ased proteins even if they like them and it can make
hem ill over a long period of time.

f your cat is already on a food when you bring it
ome and you'd like to change it, do it gradually by
dding a few bits to their old food and replacing more
nd more of the old with the new. This is best to
ninimize the chance of an upset tummy.

f you'd like to give your cat a few people treats, here
re some cat-acceptable options:

- Apples (peeled, seedless)
- Banana
- Blueberries
- Bread (cooked, not dough)
- Canned & cooked salmon and tuna (plain, not raw)
- Cheese (hard)
- Cooked chicken, turkey, and other meats (plain, not raw)

- Cucumber
- Eggs (plain, cooked)
- Mashed sweet potato
- Oatmeal
- Peas
- Pumpkin & other squash
- Spinach (if your cat doesn't have any kidney problems)

On the other hand, here are people treats your cat should avoid:

- Alcohol
- Caffeine, any
- Candy
- Chives, garlic, onions
- Chocolate
- Coconut milk
- Grapes/raisins
- Gum
- Seeds & Nuts
- Xylitol, an artificial sweetener

These aren't comprehensive lists, so look up foods before offering them to your cat.

There are a lot of choices for treating your furry friend and this is another area where you can get to know your cat better. Keep in mind that these treats can pack on pounds quickly, so avoid them if your cat is on a diet.

Your cat might also be interested in eating plants around the home or garden, but some are toxic to ats. There are large lists of plants to watch out for, but common ones include arrowhead vines, aloe vera, calla lily, Mother of Thousands or Millions, and string of pearls. If your cat shows a fascination with a particular plant, it's a good idea to check if it's toxic and move it regardless if it could be damaged.

A special note on spider plants is that they are considered toxic or nontoxic depending on your source, but they do contain compounds related to opium that have a hallucinogenic effect on your cat. If you have a spider plant and your cat keeps getting into it, it might be a good idea to find it a new spot away from your cat, put something bitter on it, or otherwise encourage your cat to find other entertainment. Not only is it hard on the plant, too much can make your cat sick.

## Potty time

Cats are almost always litterbox trained. You will have to choose a litterbox style (open, covered, large, small, or fancy with cleaning technologies) as well as a type of litter. Litters come with a plethora of options from the litter we all know to choices that reduce smell, wick moisture, clump quickly, and are even sustainable. Even with high quality litter, the litterbox should be cleaned at least daily.

It'll be best to pick this up before or along with your cat, so it can be ready when your cat comes home.

### _Do the thing, Karen._

Your cat will likely try to train you to do a thing. It's almost a guarantee with a cat since they are known for having big personalities and a list of unique preferences.

It could be less favorable things like demanding you feed them throughout the day despite being on a diet

It could be favorable things like letting you know their water bowl is empty or they want snuggles when you watch TV.

It might be oddball stuff like doing a specific dance when you feed them in a specific spot.

It could be demanding only specific people can feed them on specific days.

It could even that one specific person must pet them in one specific way when they visit.

The options only get weirder.

Just keep in mind whether you want to be "pushed around" on a topic. If you give in after an hour of yowling, do recognize this tells your cat you will eventually give in if they keep pushing. Of course, who minds having a special dance they do with a cat?

# Activity & Entertainment

Cats are intelligent animals who need something to do. For some, they're content judging you from a nearby shelf or messing with the dog, but many will benefit from having toys and something to explore. Many cat servants will buy trees to play on or small ropes and mice to play with.

On the other side of intelligence is preference. Your cat may just enjoy lying around in the boxes of these purchases and nothing more.

If you haven't kept a cat before, expect to play an exciting and sometimes expensive guessing game.

# Airing out your cat

Your cat might enjoy wandering around your home and keeping you company as you garden.

However, it's not generally a good idea to let your cat outside.

Some people have success only allowing the cat out with supervision knowing that pets in nearby yards will keep the cat in its own yard, then bringing the cat back inside with them.

It's a tricky game, but as a rule, letting your cat out unsupervised is strongly advised against. As much as the concern of your cat taking off to eat a bird exists or (for unfixed pets) mate, there is another major concern. As wildlife migrates and moves around, there is a chance your cat could be seriously injured or killed by wild predators or another loose pet.

Those who find their cat needs the fresh air have success with breezy windows and taking their cats for walks or picnics. Of course, these solutions hinge on the personality of your cat. Talk to your vet if you find this is a need that must be met since your vet may have recommendations unique to your area and cat.

# Changes in your home

Anytime you bring somebody new to your home, there will be changes. This is as true for fish and roommates as it is for a cat. These are a few common changes you'll see from a new inhabitant!

## *Crepuscular Creatures*

Despite a reputation for being active all night (your mileage may vary), cats aren't actually nocturnal (your mileage may vary). They're on a schedule called "crepuscular" where they are most active during twilight – dawn and dusk. If your sleep schedule overlaps with this range, expect the sound of cat shenanigans to wake you up on occasion. If your cat doesn't quite support your set of rules, you may also find the rule breaking happens during these times.

# The inevitable mess

All pets will make a mess, just like your roommate Doug who left spilled milk on the counter.

Common "messes" from cats include the following:

- Walking on counters right after the litterbox
- Knocking things off shelves
- Broken glass and spills (from being knocked off a surface)
- Tearing up furniture
- Climbing curtains
- Shredding carpets, rugs, paper products
- Biological messes
- Fur on anything and everything
- Inexplicable claw marks on things
- Blood spots on your clothing after you've been climbed on
- Water spills from your weird cat that enjoys self-imposed bathing
- Spills and breaks from trying to eat other pets or pests

Of course, your cat will come up with its own unique mess of some kind.

For some people, this is the nail in the coffin. They don't want their things broken, to wipe down their counters more frequently, or try to clean fur off their clothing.

For others, this are no-brainer non-issues.

### _The box conundrum_

Before bringing your cat home, examine your home
for multiple litter box spots. Your cat will need a quiet
peaceful place to potty, just like we want. However, if
your spot is subpar, your cat may find its own spot.
Plan out where to put it where it is quiet, usually dark
or not especially open, and can handle a little bit of a
smell. If possible, find several spots like this where
you and your cat can come to an agreement.

# Choosing a cat

Cats are domesticated and social animals who have a
well-earned reputation for being just as likely
persnickety and sassy as they are shy and mellow-
mannered. You should consider what kind of cat you'd
like and expect to fall in love with a completely
different kind as well.

### _Length of fur_

The length of fur is an important factor to consider. A
long-haired cat and those with thick coats (long or
short) will produce more fur. Long-haired cats will
also need brushing to keep their fur from matting and
becoming tangled.

For gorgeous locks, this is a quality over quantity
situation. There aren't a whole ton of long-hair breeds

f cat, but all of them very distinct. Here are a few
ommon options:

- Ragdoll
- Siberian
- Maine Coon
- Himalayan
- Persian
- Birman

hort hair cats don't quite look as luxurious, but they
von't need so much brushing and thinner, shorter
oats won't produce as much fur around the house
your mileage may vary).

'or these shorter coats, there's a plethora of options.
Iere are just a few short hair cats:

- Russian blue
- Bombay
- Siamese
- Chartreux
- Egyptian Mau
- Scottish fold
- Burmese

n addition, American and British shorthair breeds
ire varied and easy to find.

## Breeders or rescues

If you're absolutely sold on what exact kind of cat you want, you might find it at a rescue. You might also be stuck going with a breeder. A reputable breeder should not be a mill, will vet prospective owners, and provide your kitten with necessary vet car prior to sending them home. In general, reputable breeders will cost more than a rescue, and the cost can be shocking, so do expect to pay a significant sum more.

If you're not set on any traits or want something generic or common, try a local shelter. A good shelter or rescue will let you visit with cats and tell you anything they've noticed. For example, a rescue cat I worked with had a habit of yowling excessively at everything and letting you know his thoughts. We had no problem letting visitors know he had *opinions* (mostly because he'd let them know for us), and that cat was perfect for someone and found a home in no time. Keep in mind that, when visiting a rescue, pets have a tendency of choosing you and it's hard to go home without a pet so be ready to bring your new friend home.

## Personality

Something to keep in mind with cats is they are very human-like in their personalities. They can be loud or quiet, extroverted or introverted, timid or outgoing. These traits can also change as they grow and change or even as their environment changes from where you got them to the comfort of home. In general, you'll see

ome of who they really are crop up even when they're
n a stressful "first visit" situation.

Expect that your cat's personality is a gamble and
could potentially change in time. It's also very likely to
always be the same. If you've brought your cat home
from a shelter or similar environment, expect the
largest changes to happen then due to the stress levels
having minimized and exacerbated some traits. For
some cats, this is no change at all.

Of course, a trait like aggression toward other cats,
dogs, or children isn't likely to iron out on its own. If
you'd like a cat that will handle these situations,
choose that cat to begin with.

# Review of Cats

Cats are complicated and exciting companions to
keep! If cats appeal to you, it's best to consider the
pros and cons and the logistics of the cat you'd like to
have before bringing it home. The less chaos and last-
minute planning you both have to deal with, the less
stress. Once your cat is used to its new home, the two
of you can enjoy living together and getting used to
each other.

# Chapter 4: Barking, Meowing: Dog Husbandry

Dogs aren't just man's best friend or woman's best friend. A kind-natured dog will befriend anything from your pet lizard to the loose cricket crawling around the floor – it might also eat the cricket.

These are animals that vary so much that a lot of care choices will boil down to you and your dog.

Before bringing a dog home, it is best to scout out a vet. You'll want to know what it will cost for those annual vaccinations and exams as well as food costs. If your budget is tight, you can also find out if your area allows for you to administer your own vaccinations or visit a humane society for reduced costs.

In the last chapter for cats, we covered a few unique messes you can expect when you bring a cat home. For dogs, let's just say you can expect everything plus the unexpected, especially if you don't expect your dog to stand or climb. Once your dog is more acclimated to your home, they will respect the rules, but they are accident prone and curious, just like people.

Here are some other things to consider for bringing your pup home!

# Caring for the domesticated wolf

Dogs have a variety of needs that vary from the breed of your dog, to your home situation, to the region you live in. There are a lot of areas where the reality is, it's just best to talk to your vet. I like to compile a list of any non-pressing questions I might have for my next visit, so I don't forget or call them constantly.

When you do go to the vet, it's not just safer to use a car harness and a clip that connects to a car seat clip (or a similar feature), it can relieve anxiety. If your dog has a lot of car anxiety, try securing them in this manner so they don't slide around. They should have enough space to lie down without sliding when sitting.

For urgent matters or decisions regarding their health, it is best to talk to your vet, even if it means paying for a visit. The reason is that online discussion forums and anecdotal advice can do significantly more harm than good and be full of poorly researched myths.

If you've never had a dog before, it's normal to have a lot of health concerns as you settle into the role. It's also normal to find your dog has more and more of a personality the longer you keep them! When you enjoy their little quirks, they will pick up on it and learn to grow them!

## *Food & Water*

Your dog should always have water available, especially during times when they are stressed, it is extremely hot or cold, or they aren't feeling well. For larger dogs, a water bowl dispenser is the easiest way to keep up on this for many. It's a large container of water, like the ones in water coolers, flipped upside down over a bowl to keep it full (until the bottle runs out). Otherwise, monitor your dog's needs and consider your dog's size to pick a bowl the right size for them.

Dogs tend to get their water bowls dirty, so expect to wash it with every refill. Dogs can also go through a significant amount of water after activity or during the heat, so err on the side of a little large.

Food types are best discussed with your vet to determine what to feed them and how often. The directions on the bag aren't always a good representation of your dog's needs and can result in over- or underfeeding.

When considering a food, look over the ingredients list. Dogs are carnivores who have adapted some omnivorous habits and abilities, but they are still carnivores at the end of the day. The first ingredient on any food should be meat, and little to no corn since it's used as a filler that provides your dog little to no nutrients.

But food is where it really is between you and your vet and your dog. I've heard a lot of people who really tried to switch to expensive, well reviewed dog foods..

nd it just didn't work out. Other than just food references, allergies are a very real health concern.

)n the other side of food is treats. Dogs love treats nd you can train your dog to do nearly anything, specially food motivated dogs, with the right treats. Vhen looking at treats for dogs, they are omnivores hat err on the side of carnivores. However, saying hey're either definitely carnivores or omnivores is a opic of debate.

)ogs can derive a lot of nutrition from plant-based oods, but their bodies still need meat to thrive. )verall, dogs have more optimal features for eating neat over plants and grains, but they benefit from nd enjoy some additional sources of food!

)f course, your dog will have their own preferences, ut here are a few easy people treats your dog may njoy:

- Blueberries
- Carrots (these are great chew treats, too)
- Cheese (this should be a rare and small sized treat)
- Dog ice cream, not people ice cream
- Egg (cooked without spices or additives, minimal oils and fats, no salt)
- Freeze dried liver
- Green peas (in moderation, not canned, and only if your dog does not have kidney issues)
- Honey (just a little!)
- Lettuce (arugula, romaine, iceberg, chopped up and plain, not kale or spinach)
- Peanut butter (but not salted peanuts)

- Plain yogurt
- Popcorn (unsalted, unbuttered)
- Strawberries

Dogs can eat a huge variety of foods, but there's also a lot their bodies simply can't handle. Make sure to avoid these common foods:

- Anything with caffeine
- Chocolate
- Garlic
- Grapes
- Green tomato
- Most nuts other than peanuts
- Onion
- Potatoes

As you can see, the things to avoid are a lot shorter than things to try. Just make sure to research any snacks you offer before you put it in their bowl and keep most snacks in moderation since those pounds or otherwise negligible side effects can add up quickly.

## *Potty Time*

If you're in an apartment, consider how much you're willing to go outside. A puppy might need to go almost constantly, an adult dog won't need to go too often, and a senior could have any number of issues come up. Find a good spot near the door to set up your "going potty kit" with a leash, bags, and keys if you do not have a yard your dog can go out in! Many owners ind a simple table or coat hanger works wonders to keep things neat.

When your dog does potty, you will need to clean it up. If it's not your yard, you can use grocery bags, or you can order some online. If sustainability is your goal, you can even order compostable dog bags made from corn starch. Corn starch derived products are more compostable than some of the other "compostable" products. You will also want to find out how big the bags are, since some are best suited for small dogs only.

Always bring two more bags than you'll need.

If it is your yard, the more frequent you pick it up, the better. In the heat of the summer, each pile is a treasure to flies. I find I need to make a quick round at least daily to keep them under control. In winter and rain, it's just annoying to get it after the storm passes. Also, it can make your yard smell pretty bad.

I'd recommend a metal bin or something sturdy to the elements for keeping a bag in with a lid. For scooping, a metal two-piece scooper costs more up front, but it will handle rough weather better and is less likely to break than a plastic one-handed scooper.

Another note for your yard, female dogs squat down against the lawn to urinate. Since urine is filled with nitrogen and other compounds normally found in fertilizer, it can be a focused fertilizer overdose that "burns" that area of the lawn. This isn't something that is wrong with your dog that should be treated, it's just a side effect of nature. The best way to handle it is to spray down the area to flush the lawn and dilute the "fertilizer."

## *Activity & Entertainment*

Your dog will need stay active. This is totally dependent on your breed and your dog himself. There are breeds that are inclined to be very, very high energy and need a lot of exercise, such as most shepherds, huskies, and collies. There are also just personalities that don't really care, even within those breeds.

If you are a high activity home who loves to camp, hike, and be outdoors, look for a breed that needs high activity and can handle the weather you'd be in since some dogs really can't handle heat. If you'd rather come home and watch TV, choose a low energy dog.

Your dog will also need entertainment. This could be toys or games or puzzles or duties. Some dogs are happy to play fetch and tug. Some dogs aren't just highly intelligent, they're bred to have a purpose. For these dogs, find a job for them to do before they get bored or they'll find one.

For dogs, nearly anything can be a toy. Ropes are fun for tug of war. Tennis balls are fun for fetch and squishing. Squeaky balls made of a thick material are fun to make noise and chase. Frisbees are fun to chase.

If you'd like your dog to have stuffed toys they don't tear up, I've found toys that don't have a squeaker or plastic features do best. The squeakers obviously drive dogs crazy, but the plastic eyes and noses do as well, for some reason. I also find ears, noses, legs, and tails will get pulled off.

For maximum longevity, loaf shaped toys seem to do best.

Plush cotton stuffing is best. The pellet stuff isn't just a health concern, dogs just don't seem to like it. The material should be soft and fluffy or like denim. Dogs don't usually like felt or velvet-like materials.

I normally look at stuffed animal sections for people to get these. Just take the toy away when they start to destroy it, and they'll learn to play with it without eating them. They'll definitely get it dirty, though.

## Airing your dog out

Before you bring a dog home, check whatever you know about the breed, though this can be difficult with rescue mixes. If you can see the dog is a collie mix, prepare for the likelihood that this dog will be high energy, high intelligence and need an active home with tasks for it to complete. If you see a Great Pyrenees, expect an oddball dog that needs a short walk in cool weather.

Once you get adjusted to your dog's energy levels, make sure to walk them and hang out with them enough to wear them out. If they get bored, they'll likely start taking it out on the den. In fact, chewing up the den is one of the major symptoms of not getting enough walking and bird watching in or, otherwise, anxiety, which some activity can alleviate.

# Meeting your puppy's needs

Dogs have a variety of needs to attend to, but many of them will depend on your dog. Here are some common things your dog will need attention paid to.

## *Do the thing, Karen.*

Dogs are very adept at connecting "action" to "reward." In fact, positive reinforcement is being researched and coming out time and time again as the most effective way to train your dog. Action -> cookie / desired result is a very easy connection for your dog to make.

As a result, dogs have a habit of, in a way, training us.

It might be that you take them potty every time you si down to dinner.

It might be that knocking your phone out of your han means they get attention.

It might be that sitting between you and your view of the TV means pets o'clock.

It might be a detailed happy dance when you get home.

It might be that rubbing their elbows into sensitive areas earns them pets.

It might be that putting their snout next to your plate and drooling a little earns a little snack.

It might be relentlessly harassing you at 4 AM until you get up for breakfast.

It might be that barking at you beginning at 5:37 PM gets dinner in the bowl at 6:00 PM on the dot.

Worst, it might be that barking for long enough about whatever it is will get them the thing, and you *will* eventually cave.

One of my dogs has even figured out that hitting and kicking us will result in a blanket being put over her. She now does this when she is cold.

Another dog loves to game the system. During potty training, she'd pretend to potty about ten times in a trip to get extra cookies. Later, she'd learn to go outside just to get a cookie for returning.

It's important to keep in mind what your dog sees as far as "action > result" when you cave to demands. Dogs need consistency to speak our language.

Not only do you need to be consistent with your dog, guests and house members do, too. Get everybody on the same page, and your dog will follow suit.

Otherwise, your dog will end up having certain people they have trained to accept bad habits.

## *Now you do the thing, Spot.*

While nearly any pet can be trained, dogs aren't only good at accepting it, we've also gotten good at offering it. There is an unfathomable amount of resources available to dog owners today, some great, some good some not so good.

Overall, we know that dogs are best trained with positive enforcement. It's the same type of treatment that works with people, too. If your boss gave you one of your favorite treats every time you did an unfavorable task, you might be first in line to do it. If your boss only reprimanded you when you messed up but gave you a gentle pat on the back for your unfavorable task, you would only work to avoid a reprimanding and little else.

Positive reinforcement in dogs is accomplished by rewarding an action or choice within 6 seconds of it happening since your dog will not make the connection once their focus has changed. Unlike your boss rewarding you, your dog won't understand "Great job on that sitting project last month, here's an entire jar of peanut butter."

Dogs can only make the instant connection.

For example, if your dog sits on command, and it takes ten seconds to finagle the cookie from the cooki pouch and your dog is now chasing leaves, they will assume they are getting a cookie for chasing leaves. They need to come and sit again to get their cookie.

You can also create a consistent association between "action" and "word." Every time your dog sits, it's not just ambiguous "good" (HAPPY VOICE), it's "sit" (HAPPY VOICE). Cookies definitely make this a more exciting event as well. In time, your dog will hear "sit" and know that sit is a HAPPY HUMAN event.

On the other side of things, your dog can associate "action" to "outcome" in a negative way just as easily. If your dog is off digging up your neighbor's new rose bush and you call them, but they wait until the bush is dead to come to you, the action is no longer "BUSH DIGGING" but "COME." Obviously, you are frustrated. Your neighbor is a rare rose bush connoisseur and that bush is your entire month's income.

However, all your dog knows is they have "COME." If your dog comes to your feet and sits, but you are angry because you cannot pay your bills now, your dog will see "COME" as an ANGRY HUMAN event. You especially do not want your dog to be afraid of coming to you.

So, while "action" and "outcome" are easy connections, it is only for a moment. As soon as their attention has changed, the "action" being applied to the result changes.

In other words, we ignore the bad behavior.

At least, once the moment is passed.

If your dog is in the process of being a mischievous dog or considering it, a startling sound, a defined sound or noise to the effect of "no, bad dog" (some trainers recommend hissing like a snake, which I have found to be really effective), or marching toward them with your hands down are all effective ways of telling them to knock it off.

Continue to approach them until they have retreated from the action. If they won't drop the topic, get between them and the object. If they still won't drop it, remove the dog to another area for a time out where they must relax (this should not be the kennel). Some trainers leash the dog and hold them close until the dog relaxes. They will quickly learn the escalation pattern to "boring time out."

For example, if your dog is bringing their nose toward that vine you just planted, they need to turn away from it completely. If they look ready to get back to it the second you turn away, they haven't retreated from the action.

Once they do retreat, drop the interaction immediately. If you continue, they will no longer understand why you're upset.

Overall, this is all the things your dog has trained you to do, in reverse. Every time they want attention, they simply need to power land on your stomach and you know to pet them. If you don't, they "help" you understand until you do. We just have to do it in a kinder, less organ crushing manner.

You will also want to integrate breaks into training time. More than fifteen minutes or so will reduce the effectiveness of your sessions, so take plenty of breaks to refresh!

If you find you and your dog aren't quite on the same wavelength, you can reach out to a vet or a dog trainer. The best dog trainers are known from taking a household in chaos to a peaceful home.

If you'd like to see how fast and clear positive reinforcement can be and your dog likes to bite your hand for cookie time, train them to be easy.

Have them sit while you hold a cookie tightly in your fingers. Slowly bring it to them. Every time they jump toward you, pull your hand back. Begin to offer it again only when they have returned to a relaxed position.

Keep offering and pulling it back as soon as they move until they can accept it without jumping or biting. This is hardest as you get to their mouth and they may bite your fingers. Do not drop the treat but pull it back quickly. If your dog successfully bites you at any point, yelp when you pull away.

If you're tired of trying, put the cookie away as soon as the bite occurs and return to this lesson later. However, I've never had this be an issue. Most dogs will get the message very quickly.

If you make a habit of every cookie being offered only to a sitting, gentle dog, your dog will habitually stop biting, even with strangers.

Apply this concept of doing the good thing (not biting or jumping) and get a good thing (the cookie) to anything you'd like your dog to understand. Start very easy and move up from there. For example, 'heel', 'stay', and 'come' should begin in a small room, then throughout the house, then in larger environments until they are second nature.

# Choosing a dog

What dog you choose is ultimately up to you barring local laws or contracts you've signed with your landlord or HoA. Make sure everything is clear for any laws you've agreed to adhere to, and you may literally have your pick of the litter.

## ***Long hair, short hair; Big dog, little dog; High energy, low energy***

Consider what kind of traits you don't only admire but *want to keep*.

First, what kind of dogs do you like? Do you want (and can keep) a *big* dog? How big is big to you? 60lb (27kg), like a small retriever, Bassett Hound, or a Chow Chow? 90lb (40kg), like an Akita, Bernese, or Doberman Pinscher? Or a giant at 110lb (50kg) and up, like a Great Dane, Mastiff, Pyrenees, or St. Bernard?

Many larger dogs will be more costly to feed, but not all. Some large dogs are meant to be sedentary and have low metabolisms.

Or do you want a *little* dog? How little is little to you? About 5lb (2kg) like a toy Chihuahua or Papillion? 10lb (4.5kg) like a Miniature Pinscher? Closer to 20lb (9kg) like a Shiba Inu or Corgi?

A small dog may still have a high metabolism and need regular exercise. Some corgis, for example, fall into the "small dog" range, but they are herding dogs that need frequent exercise.

Do you want a medium dog, somewhere in between, like some terriers or shepherds?

If energy levels are a concern for you, especially if you are meeting a mix, make sure to ask when meeting a prospective dog. There is always an exception! Some Australian shepherds end up being couch potatoes, and some Saint Bernards want to go adventuring constantly! You're more likely to find dogs follow their breed's tendencies, though.

Long hair dogs require more brushing to keep their fur free of matting and tangling even if they don't shed as much as you'd expect. Short hair dogs won't mat as much but they might still shed a lot – Labradors, for example, are known for shedding constantly even with brushing.

Long hair dogs will also need more bathing since their long furs can trap dirt and dust. Short hair coats will require less bathing. For coats like a Labrador's, some owners find their dogs never *need* a bath in the lifetime even if they still get a few.

If you're looking at a breed, research what kind of habits they have before you go out to get one.

## *Breeder vs. Rescue*

There's a lot of debate between going to a breeder or getting a rescue with dogs. Some groups even see it as shameful to get a dog from a breeder.

Ultimately, it's up to you.

There's a reason that breeders exist. Purebreds often have a purpose or demand that breeders are striving to meet. Working dogs are bred to continue and encourage favorable traits, and show dogs are bred for aesthetic and personality. Regardless, a responsible breeder will breed for health above everything.

You'll find the following with a responsible breeder:

- Fewer litters from a dog and only up to a certain age (for the mother's health)
- The parents will not have common issues found in the breed (e.g. no hip dysplasia in large breed dogs)
- The first round of shots, at least, for puppies (and records for this)
- Puppies that, other than obvious sources (such as being brought outside to play and promptly rolling in dirt), are clean and well kept

- Puppies that won't be sent home earlier than 7 or 8 weeks.
- Puppies that are kept in their home and socialized well with people
- At least the mother on site (some breeders might hire a vetted sire rather than keep him on site)
- The breeder will have a method to determine if you will provide a good home
- The breeder will offer to take their puppy back if you decide you don't want it
- A hefty fee! Responsible breeding is costly and many just break even, if that, and in-demand breeders will often raise prices rather than increasing production

On the other hand, you can rescue a dog. Rescuing a dog carries a mixed reputation, as well. On the other side of unscrupulous breeders is unscrupulous rescues that aren't honest about a dog's situation. People hear or experience stories like discovering the dog has heart worms and the rescue knew, a diagnosis that isn't just difficult and life threatening but costly. The dog might also not be house trained, or it might be aggressive.

When you're looking at a rescue, look for some signs of a more reliable rescue:

- A vetting process, sometimes more intensive than your emotionally attached breeder, because they do not want to see the rescue return another time.
- Honest information about the animals such as "Needs to be the only dog in the house" or

"Working on potty training." These aren't helpful for moving the dog, but it will save it the heartbreak of a bad placement.

- Health information. Some rescues won't place a dog who is facing a major health issue. If they can, they bring their dogs to reputable vets to ensure they are in good health. Regardless, they should let you know of any concerns they have.

- A great reputation. Rescues move a lot of animals, even small ones with extended vetting processes and high fees. If the reputation is that they're too hard to adopt from, that's different than hiding things to get a dog to move. These rescues will also come with numerous recommendations.

Wherever you choose to bring your dog home from, they're your new best friend, and you've made the best decision you can for the both of you!


## *Personality*

Like cats, dogs are as different from each other as people are. If you're looking at a puppy from any source, recognize its personality can grow and change as the puppy grows. It also might not. Most puppies I've seen grow have had the same core personality as the day they were brought home. I've also seen dogs that experienced something traumatic or not that caused their personalities to do a 180.

Regardless, expect your dog to have a personality. The more you talk to, engage, and involve your dog, the more you'll see who they are and the more they'll be comfortable telling you their thoughts.

Keep this in mind when you feel silly talking to your dog. They love it. They want to be part of your thought process and day.

The best part of their personality is it will give you cues for when things are hard. My dogs like to be included so much that, when they are upset over a mild wind or thunderstorm, I can read them a picture book, and they will forget there's a storm.

Like cats, aggression issues aren't always likely to go away. If you want a dog that handles cats, dogs, or children, choose a dog that is good with these situations to begin with.

# Review of Dogs

Dogs are an interesting, highly domesticated, highly intelligent, and highly hilarious species. Despite being considered one of the highest care common pets, 89 million dogs found their place in Americans' homes in 2017, so we must find their companionship worth it.

Once you prepare your home and decide what dog to bring home, you can move onto enjoying your new venting buddy! You'll start to discover little traits like the face they make when you try to sing, or their unbridled enthusiasm over their favorite activity.

# Chapter 5: Chirping, Crunching: Husbandry for the Humble Insect

Invertebrates exist in absolutely any environment on earth, and their care can be simple or extremely difficult. It's a massive term and group with miscellaneous creatures that tend to get lumped in as "insects." This chapter is dedicated to the care of insects and what we colloquially and not officially refer to as insects. By that, I mean creatures like spiders which are not *technically* insects (an argument a screaming person does not care to hear). Still, their care is very similar.

## The Natural Insect Habitat

Insects fit into a myriad of niches and, ugh, homes throughout the world. Any bug, depending on the situation, can be a pest, neutral, or even beneficial. So when we consider their care, we are thinking about something that doesn't demand as much active attention personally as much as attention to their habitats and needs. Once you find this balance, your insects will usually be very happy!

The hardest part about bringing home an insect is that, once you nail down that environmental balance, it's easy to bring home a hundred more.

Here are those environments we usually create for insects as pets!

# Grains and Flours

Some insects lay their eggs in grains, and this is both their environment and sustenance. In this case, we're usually growing the larvae or keeping it fed as food. Superworms, mealworms, and rice beetle larvae are the most common type of insect kept in this environment!

Insects kept in grains and flours are happy to live in a tub or ventilated container of any sort, just as they would in the wild. The wild being your old bag of flour.

These larvae ask for care in the form of the occasional vegetable such as lettuce or potatoes and a nutritious, sometimes supplemented, mix of corn, rice and wheat flours.

These insects shouldn't be provided direct moisture. At most, a vegetable snack will be more than plenty. Otherwise, the grains can mold and invite harmful pests.

# Soils, trees, caves, and fruits

A high-quality soil made of decaying matter and bark, or other decaying woods, meets the needs of countless insects that convert decaying matter like leaves and woods into nutritious soil for plants. These types of insects make great roommates in a vivarium, but the soil will need to be replaced more frequently since it is their source of food.

In breeding insects, these habitats are easy to maintain by simply filling a tub with this soil, adding holes for ventilation, and maintaining temperature, humidity, and fresh soil to munch.

This also works for worms. Worms used for compost are simply kept in a deep container with decaying fruits and vegetables that they turn into nutritious soil additions!

Some insects are specialized to break down decaying fruits. This might overlap into a variety of grubs, larvae, and small insects in the soil that eat fallen and rotten fruits, but it can also apply to something specialized like fruit flies. In general, fruit flies are a pest. As hobbyists, flightless fruit flies are rarely successful home invaders outside of their containers but excellent sources of nutrition for small insects and animals.

Other than decaying matter, some pets such as tarantulas just want something to climb on or burrow under. They may enjoy bark and sticks to climb on, but they will also be happy with the right soil to walk on or burrow into.

Burrowing insects will need deep enough soil to burrow into.

Terrestrial insects don't need more than a comfortable layer of soil, but they do want something to hide in. A piece of cork bark cut in half is an attractive and common choice, but anything they can hide under and call safe is a good choice.

For insects that don't eat the soil, simply choose a soil they won't accidentally swallow and get sick from when they eat. Coco fiber is a common choice, but there are special soil mixes as well. Replace these soils every few weeks and spot clean the soil and enclosure.

## _Water and air_

Some insects live in extremely wet conditions, and some buzz through the air. Not a lot of dedicated flyers and swimmers are kept as a hobby. Those that need to fly will need a lot of space, while those that fly by chance don't seem to mind too much either way. Those that live in water are rarely interesting pets that have complicated needs.

These insects are usually accommodated in individual containers short term for the purpose of feeding other insects or animals.

On the other hand, some insects like air space because they are arboreal. For these insects, something to climb and lord over their enclosure is a must. Tall enclosures with coco fiber substrate, a stick to stand on, and maybe some fake plants or flowers is a good habitat.

## A Plethora of Options

Now that we know what kind of habitats we can provide, let's look at the insects we can keep!

## _Ants_

This is a whole different can of worms, but it is a growing hobby. For ants, you are keeping an entire colony susceptible to pests and predators even within your terrarium.

I'd recommend some experience handling terrariums or buying a kit for beginners.

AntsCanada.com and AntsKingdom.com offer more considered kits and resources, even a book, for those looking to enter this hobby. In addition, there are a lot of resources on this if you haven't seen much on ant keeping before.

## _"Clean-up crew"_

Many vivarium keepers are enjoying having insects that help turn waste into quality soil. These insects include springtails, isopods, and millipedes. In general, these helpers are pretty harmless. They don't bite, sting or, short of signaling a problem in your home, infest a home.

These insects need moist, decaying substances to thrive. This includes oak leaves, sphagnum moss, and wood. Beyond this, they don't ask for much. Millipedes (except for those more prone to terrestrial habits over burrowing) and isopods might be more interested in exploring their environment for the sake of it and may appreciate more height and objects to

xplore, but they can also survive in more compact
ituations.

pringtails are almost always offered in a white
ariety and aren't always a notable feature of a
ivarium, but they are indispensable helpers. You can
usually find a starter culture from reptile supply
tores.

sopods aren't out and about very often, especially in
ery large vivariums, but they do come fun varieties
nd morphs! There are varieties that can get pricy
and they'll sell out), and you'll of course need a good
andful to start a colony. For more common varieties
f solid colors and common patterns, these can be
ound for a reasonable price for an entire starter
olony. These are also found at reptile supply stores.

he easiest to care for and easiest to find millipede
arieties are bumblebee, scarlet, smoky ghost, ivory,
nd Sonoran Desert. Any of these are happy with
ubstrate and even some fruit to munch on now and
hen, but I have found they do enjoy having the space
o explore and march their feet around. These are
rowing in favor for being good at helping the soil just
s much as being a pet to enjoy, so you can find them
t a lot of reptile stores.

## The Fascinating Beetle

Beetles come in a huge variety! They often aren't very
ong-lived, or those that are spend a long time being
rubs. Beetle keeping all on its own is a huge hobby

and aren't always sold at reptile stores. If you're interested in keeping a beetle, you might need to go to reptile and insect expos featuring beetles or online. Keep in mind that importing or exporting beetles between countries is not legal without extensive licensing and testing. So, it'll be cheapest and easiest to keep beetles native to your country.

In the U.S., blue death feigning beetles and Gymnetis thula are common and easy beetles.

Gymnetis thula (flower scarabs) are somewhat short lived and easy care. These harlequin flower beetles are sap-eating beetles in the wild. They spend their grub-hood in soil eating decaying wood, leaves, and apples. When they mature into beetles, they prefer to eat fruit and beetle jelly. They are small beetles that don't need much space and can be housed in groups. They will enjoy soil to walk on and space to move about but do expect them to breed if the soil is high quality and deep. These beetles do best in high humidity environments where their yellow pattern begins to darken.

Rhinoceros beetles are another scarab with somewhat easy care. They also grow in composting soil and fruits. In the U.S., these are most commonly sold as Dynastes tityus (Eastern U.S. species) or Dynastes granti (Western U.S. species). As adults, they eat fruit and beetle jellies. The care of these fun beetles is loved and researched enough there is a book on it, "The Complete Guide to Rearing the Eastern Hercules Beetle and Other Rhinocerus Beetles" by Orin McMonigle.

Blue death feigning beetles are a hardy species of darkling beetles that only need to be feed carrots, crushed dog or cat food, and veggies. They might also appreciate some things to hide under.

## The Incredible Spider and Praying Mantis

Tarantulas and praying mantids are carnivores whose care can overlap in a few ways.

Very small tarantulas and praying mantids will enjoy eating pinhead crickets and flightless fruit flies. Larger ones will enjoy eating crickets. They will both enjoy the occasional bit of variety.

Mantids are almost always arboreal ambush predators. Mantids enjoy honey as a rare treat. Mantids are also a very large group, and you should research the type you like before you bring it home. Ghost mantids are an easy and stunning species for beginners.

Tarantulas can be burrowing, terrestrial, or arboreal. Beginners are recommended to look for a new world species of tarantula, since they are less aggressive and would rather run or use their urticating hairs before biting you with venom that doesn't bother most people. It's easier for a beginner to accidentally push an Old World tarantula too far and earn a bite with venom that humans do feel.

The green bottle blue tarantula is a stunning New World tarantula for a beginner.

Most tarantulas and praying mantids should be kept solitary.

In general, if you don't need to be handling your insects, they would appreciate it if you didn't. Do be careful with handling tarantulas, especially large non arboreal types, as they can be seriously injured with a small fall.

## The weird and wacky

Insects only get odder and more interesting from here. The vinegaroon is a prime example. A mild-mannered burrowing scorpion with a flat whiptail is enough to scare plenty away, but their charm doesn't fall flat on many hobbyists these days. These are hardy, docile, long-lived species that are easy to keep.

The longer you keep insects, the more interesting things you'll see, but this should cover most insects you can find without too much digging, literally and metaphorically.

# Foods

Since insects can eat a large variety of things, we'll just go over a quick overview of options. Depending on your particular insect, there might be special foods or treats you can offer as well.

## _Beetle jellies_

These sweet treat cups are designed just for fruit-eating rhino beetles. They're fairly inexpensive when keeping just a few beetles and provide all of the nutrients your beetle will need. They're also known for rarely molding so they can stay in an enclosure for a long time before being removed.

If you keep a number of insects that can eat these or you can't get your hands on beetle jelly, you can also make your own. There are several recipes among hobbyists for this, and some of them are specialized for the type of beetles, ants, or other insects you might keep. Do know that the homemade versions don't quite last as long and must be refrigerated for storage.

## _Crickets_

Crickets are a staple food since they can be so small or somewhat large. Crickets can be "pinhead" (about the size of a pinhead) for a baby mantid or as big as about an inch (2.5cm) for larger insects like a full-grown tarantula.

Try not to feed more than your pet will eat in a short period of time since some crickets can be aggressive and harass your pet.

We'll cover more details for crickets in Chapter 7: Reptiles.

## *Decaying matter*

Decaying matter is a mix including sphagnum moss, oak leaves, and white woods. For some insects, this might need to be fermented. I'd recommend buying a high-quality mix, especially if it's offered as an option with your insect purchase, before trying to make your own. Seeing what it should look like and include makes mixing your own much, much easier.

## *Fruit*

Fruit is just that. In general, if it's starting to mold, you'll want to remove it from the enclosure, though I've caught my millipedes and isopods munching down the mold. If they've kept it under control, you can leave it in. Otherwise, take it out before it negatively impacts their health.

Feed fruits like cantaloupe, apples, pears and bananas. Avoid offering citrus since this is hard on many insects unless yours is known to accept it.

## Fruit flies

Fruit flies are a fantastic source of nutrition for smaller insects. Your baby tarantula or mantid may require these and love them at that age, but as they grow, they will stop chasing after them. Up to that point, offer them whatever they'll eat and enjoy the baby years!

Fruit flies are sold in cups with premixed food and excelsior, or wood wool, to climb on and about.

Some reptile stores will offer kits with a powder mix to make your own culture, which is much cheaper than buying the cup every time. In this case, just follow the directions to mix the powder with water in the cup, top it with excelsior, and add adult fruit flies. Wait about two weeks for them to produce and grow a new culture. You can continue this indefinitely if they are kept up.

# Review of insects

Insects are fun and varied pets that can fit into nearly any hobbyist's home. Once you decide what kind of habitat you'd like to keep, it's easy to pick an insect. With how easy many insects are, it's almost as easy to pick an insect before deciding what habitat to set up!

# Chapter 6: Itsy-Bitsy and Invisible: Microscopic Husbandry

Some pets aren't very visible, but they're just as fun to keep. This chapter is just a quick review of these small pets and their simple care!

## Kinds of microscopic pets

There are mainly two common types of pets that are kept in this category. At least, intentionally. Both can used for food, especially when splitting their cultures!

### *Yeast*

Bakers rejoice and groan in the option to grow their own yeast. Yeast cultures produce sourdough, favored for its tangy flavor and ease of care.

Not actually an animal, yeast is a single-celled organism in the fungi kingdom. Yeast is so easy to find that it turns out it's just one fungus of many among us in the air. When having people over, you can invite them to meet a real fungi!

Yeast is easy to start in your own kitchen for the cost of its food and isn't something you must purchase a culture to start! King Arthur Flour isn't just one of the main sources for these instructions, they have a site dedicated to articles and recipes for bakers. If you're just starting out, this is a huge resource.

For keeping yeast and baking sourdough, you'll want a scale and reliable kitchen thermometer to produce the best environment for these microbes.

## Algae & Co.

Algae is a more generic option for a pet, and also not part of the animal kingdom. Nonetheless, these pets can inspire joy and require some special care. Some algaes, like spirulina, are grown for food. Other algae, like Pyrocystis cultures, are marine cultures admired for their bioluminescence.

Spirulina is a cyanobacteria and is taxonomically not at all algae, but its algae-like habits have us all calling it algae. Aquarists may spend their lives fighting the cyanobacteria, but this cyanobacterium is lauded for its nutrition and ease of care. Many algae supply stores offer these cultures.

Pyrocystis is a marine dinoflagellate. These fascinating phytoplankton have a special ability: They can glow in the dark! In the day, their cell structures change to photosynthesize and produce energy and the chemicals necessary for bioluminescence such as luciferase. Compared to a firefly, the luciferase of these dinoflagellates is very short-lived and only momentarily observable. The bioluminescence is produced for a second or a few (depending on the species and strength of the culture) when the culture is agitated.

Some science and algae supply stores offer Pyrocystis cultures. You can get P. fusiformis, P. noctiluca, and P. lunula. They all have minimally different habits and colors, and any should work. I did find Carolina Biological Supply sometimes offers the all three species, though.

# Where to keep your pet (and never see it)

### *Yeast*

Starting a culture is easy (except for when it's not). First, source out your flour. You'll want whole rye, whole wheat, or unbleached all-purpose flour. Rye is the recommended starting flour, and any mixture of the above unbleached flours is fine in any combination for feeding.

Once you choose your flour and container (usually a jar, but anything food safe should work), mix 1-part flour to 1-part water by weight. Keep your culture in an area where it is about 70°F (21°C). Too cold and it won't flourish, too warm and it will consume its resources too quickly, and over 95°F (35°C), it can die

Every day remove ½ of your starter and replace it with the amount you removed. If your starter is 200g then you will discard 100g of it and add 50g of flour and 50g of water.

After about two weeks of this, give or take a few days, your yeast culture will outcompete other microbes and it should smell like sourdough! Best of all, it should be doubling in size and full of bubbles, ready to lift your baked goods or split into more cultures.

If this isn't quite working out, you want to avoid dealing with this, or you'd like to see what another culture tastes like, some sourdough bakeries sell starters. King Arthur Flour and San Francisco sourdough bakeries are popular choices, but there are many options.

A debate among bakers is whether buying a culture from another source tastes different permanently from a culture started in your kitchen, or if it becomes the wild type in your region after a few feedings. If you buy one, feel free to keep an eye on the flavor to see if you feel like it ever changes!

And yes, it is normal to name your culture!

## *Pyrocystis*

For Pyrocystis, I found care sheets were sparse and not always thorough. I've had long-term success with mish-mashing some tips here and there together.

You'll want a strong, full-spectrum light. A small but high-quality aquarium light that will cover the size of your set up. If you have only a few, you should only need about 12" (30cm) to 24" (60cm) coverage, at most.

Choose a fairly shady spot in your home where the direct sunlight will not burn your cultures and you can get to a dark space or make it a dark space. Pyrocystis should also be kept right around room temperature.

Your light should run for 12 hours on a timer. Choose a period of time when you won't be trying to view them, and they have 2 hours to transition from their photosynthesizing "daytime" period to their bioluminescent "nighttime" period. Your cultures will not light up until at least 2 hours after "night" has begun. My preferred schedule for the light to run is 8 PM to 8 AM, but you can adjust this to your preference.

Your cultures will do well in an Erlenmeyer flask with stoppers. These cultures would not fair well in an aquarium or in an open container, as they are very edible, and their water quality will be as well.

Fill your flasks to be about 125ml salt water and 125m existing/new culture.

About every 2-4 weeks, the cultures will begin to deteriorate. You can feed them now or even a little earlier. Simply remove about half the culture and refil it with water and fertilizer. Give them a few days to a week to recover before you'll see them begin returning to full strength.

If your Pyrocystis culture (a chunkier, more brown colored algae) is developing a green algae problem, change the cultures more frequently, closer to every week or two, until the Pyrocystis is able to outcompete the other algae. A pipette can also help spot clean the green algae. In general, if my Pyrocystis is happy, there isn't any green algae, and a happy Pyrocystis culture seems to just look like dirty water.

During their "night" period, simply shake the flash to see your Pyrocystis light up! When I keep my flasks fuller, I have noticed P. lunula tends to stick around the edges of the flask and continue bumping into each other and sparkling long after I've shaken the container. It makes the pretty minimal care this pet takes worthwhile!

## Spirulina

Spirulina is kept inside a translucent container such as a large jar or a small aquarium. Either place it by a window with a lot of light or under grow lights. Fill your container with water, and if your home is room temperature, add a heater to raise the temperature to 89-98°F (32-37°C). Use Litmus paper or another pH test to test your water, you want the pH to be 8-8.5. If it's too low, add baking soda. If it's too high, add vinegar.

Once your water is just right, add your Spirulina starter culture to its new home. Keep it stirred or use an air pump to keep the culture moving. As the water evaporates or some is removed, make sure to keep it topped off to keep your culture in tip-top shape.

Over time, it'll raise the pH of your water. Once the pH is over 10, you can harvest it by removing some and straining out the water!

# What to feed the invisible

## _Grains_

Yeast should be fed and started with unbleached grains, since the bleaching process removes yeast and some of the nutrients it needs. Unbleached all-purpose flour, whole grain flours, and rye are the most popular options.

Yeast will munch on nearly any grain you want to give it, but keep in mind anything you feed it will be in the final product that you bake. So, if you don't like rye or the flavor it imparts, use only some or none in your feedings. However, rye is very tasty and nutritious for yeast.

If you have a store that sells a variety of grain flours in bulk, you can buy a small portion of many and see what you and your culture like best! Each flour will cause your culture to taste a little different.

Shy away from nut flours as the oils in them can cause your culture to go rancid or develop a rancid flavor.

## _Fertilizer_

When growing algae, there are a few options. For many algae, Guillard's f/2 formulation is best and made specifically for algae. This is the easiest fertilizer to offer your Pyrocystis. Simply follow the included directions to make a f/2 dilution. Do not increase the concentration, as doubling it makes it an f/1 ormulation and this can be too much for your Pyrocystis to live in.

For Spirulina, there are many options for fertilizer available ranging from homemade to specialized formulas.

## Water

Some sourdough keepers find their water is hard on their yeast and have better success with mineral or distilled waters. However, most safe to drink tap waters should be more than fine.

For Spirulina, any safe to drink water that results in a high pH for the starter culture is good.

For Pyrocystis, clean marine water is the most important part for this organism. If you have a local fish store nearby that has pristine marine tanks, you can usually buy pre-mixed salt water to make your media from. A gallon or two is usually more than enough for them for a couple months of changes. Since nature finds a way, I usually inspect the water before use as well and replace it if it looks questionable. If you're feeling questionable about this option, you can buy pre-mixed media just for pyrocystis, sometimes with algae food pre-mixed in, but it will cost a lot more once it's shipped.

## _Light_

In general, sourdough doesn't really need light. It's happy to grow in its food-safe container. Translucent containers are nice for watching the bubbles, though.

Spirulina can be kept with just sunlight from a nearby window or indirect sunlight outside just as well as using grow lights. Just make sure it doesn't get over 104°F (40°C).

Pyrocystis has varying results with sunlight and sometimes doesn't handle the warmth well. It's best to use a high quality, full spectrum grow light or aquarium light for your Pyrocystis. Choose a light without a blue spectrum (like those made for saltwater) or it can encourage the wrong bacteria.

# Review of Microscopic Pets

Each of these pets may seem intimidating at first, but once you understand the care, you'll find they're pretty low maintenance. Yeast's daily changes can take only a couple minutes, spirulina can keep itself going as long as you keep an eye on it, and Pyrocystis only asks for quick maintenance every few weeks.

If you've thought about keeping a microscopic pet but worried it would be too complicated or time intensive, I hope this shows you how easy it can be!

# Chapter 7: Slithering, Pattering Reptiles

Reptiles exist in every biome, and at any height. These ectothermic creatures climb trees, relax by or in the water, and even burrow. In every corner of the world, you'll find unique and exciting reptiles that call it home.

## Reptiles all the world over and their environments

In the wild, reptiles share homes with amphibians, so you'll likely find most habitats you already have for an amphibian may just need minor tweaking for a reptile. Here are the most common habitats.

### *Paludarium*

Paludariums are covered more in depth in Chapter 1: Amphibians, with a water and possible waterfall portion as well as a land portion. These enclosures can be tall or short.

For a reptile, a paludarium mostly looks the same. The only considerations are lighting and the reptile's skills.

For example, a semi-aquatic turtle could do well in a paludarium set up right for it. Unlike an amphibian, however, a turtle will still need UVA/B lighting. In this case, the lid must not be glass, or it can trap heat and overheat your turtle and the glass will filter out the UV. If you have a pet that needs UVA/B in a paludarium, you'll not only need to include these lights but change to a screen top that can ventilate air and help regulate the temperature as well as allow UV to pass through.

Other reptile considerations include if the reptile is a good swimmer. For example, a crested gecko loves a humid environment, but some are terrible swimmers who don't deal well with a pool of water. I've witnessed these geckos, on several occasions, try to find safety in the water portion and burrow into corners until they got stuck. Some reptiles are best left out of this habitat.

## *Terrarium*

Your standard terrarium style enclosure is much like the one discussed more in depth in Chapter 1: Amphibians with a flat bottom and misting and water bowls used as a water source rather than a full water feature. These enclosures can be tall or short. It is usually very similar to a paludarium without the water feature. These enclosures are often high humidity but can just as easily meet lower humidity needs.

This type of terrarium meets the needs of burrowers, terrestrial types, and climbers.

Like the paludarium as well, this type of enclosure may need to consider that many reptiles need UVA/B exposure in addition. Some don't, like the crested gecko, but many still will.

## Desert

There are two types of desert enclosures.

There is the rocky desert featuring a sandy-pebble substrate with the option of some live plants (shy away from spiky plants if your reptile is soft-bodied) like sedum and aloe. These enclosures can be decorated with wood and rocks. Rocks should be secured via non-toxic adhesives or bolts to prevent them from shifting and injuring your pet.

There is also the sandy desert enclosure, using a sandy substrate. You can use calcium-based sand or very fine sand from a hardware store for this substrate. Fill a bucket with the sand and water and dump out the excess water and refill it until the water is clear and free of dust and dirt. Spread your sand out, preferably somewhere hot like under the sun, and allow it to dry back out.

These enclosures will need lighting that provides UVA/B as well as a significant amount of heat, up to 120°F (49°C) for some species. Place your lighting at a far end of the enclosure to create a gradient. These full-spectrum, high powered lights should run for 12-14 hours a day. Check your pet's needs to determine which type of lighting and how long they will need.

Because the desert biomes are so hot, place a cave or other option to hide under in the cooler end of the enclosure.

For humidity, a bowl just small enough to drink from but not submerge themselves in is enough for hydration. You can also pipe a small amount of water into the sand or mist the cave for extra humidity. However, this type of enclosure is better without too much humidity.

## _A bin_

Some people keep their snakes in a simple bin, tub, or rack system. Since some snakes are nocturnal and live in burrows and caves, they may never see the sun and need much for UVA/B exposure. They also feel most secure in these closed spaces they're best adapted to. If you're considering a snake that will do well in this type of enclosure, just make sure there is ventilation and the container should be large enough for the snake to comfortably fit in.

While these enclosures are a large contrast to other reptile habitats, they are usually the most comfortable for many snakes and result in happier, healthier pets. As far as replicating a natural environment for your pet, this is actually the closest many snakes can get in captivity.

# Your home

Some reptiles are active and grow large enough a simple enclosure will not be enough. They will do best with the ability to roam in your house. Commonly, these are the iguanas, monitors, or tegus. Consider the full-grown size of a reptile before bringing it home and if you want it as a roommate.

Savannah Monitors and some Tegus are enjoyed as housemates for their fun personalities, with the Savannah Monitor strongly resembling a dog. On the other hand, Iguanas tend to be very aggressive and make poor housemates, thus poor pets.

Turtles and tortoises can also get extremely large with a very long lifespan.

# Reptile options in abundance

Since reptiles are found everywhere in the world, you'll always have another one to consider! It's unreasonable to list all options, so here are just a few fun ones!

## Easy, Easy, EASY Reptiles

For an easy, easy, EASY reptile, consider the crested gecko. These arboreal lizards are smooth skinned and will do best in a temperate terrarium with a lot of height and things to climb on. They are generally laid back and will do well with handling.

These geckos do *not* require UVA/B when fed the proper diet. In the wild, they eat fruit and insects. Their diet in captivity can be as simple as a pre-mixed food for which there are a few respected brands and a well as few smaller scale mixes on the market. These mixes contain all their nutritional needs.

Crested geckos do best in high humidity environments.

The hardest care I've encountered with this pet is figuring out which mix they like best, and they simply won't eat ones they don't like.

They can also snack on small insects.

Once thought extinct, the crested gecko is still endangered in its native habitat. However, they are easy to appease in captivity and are easy to find bred in captivity.

The only major issue for many reptile keepers is the frustration of these geckos dropping their tails at the drop of a hat, since their tails won't grow back. You can buy ones that have already dropped their tail and never experience the horror of this.

# Interesting, but difficult

Chameleons, hearty insectivores, are popular and breed well in captivity, so it's easy to fall prey to their charms and find one (or a lot) for sale. However, they really are more difficult to care for, with care like more difficult orchids.

They need high humidity, from humidifiers and/or misting, with air circulation, or they can develop life-threatening health issues.

They need a lot of height and plants and vines, fake or not, to climb on to keep them entertained and hidden.

They need good lighting and supplements to support their nutritional needs.

They need moving water to keep up on their hydration, as they won't drink still water.

They are sit-and-wait predators that don't like to be exposed, so handling them isn't good for many of them. Some socialize well, but for many, it is simply stressful.

Females are likely to have shorter life spans as they can become egg bound.

Room temperature, on the other hand, is good for them as long as they have a warm basking spot.

If you get the proper enclosure and equipment to begin with, you can fall into the routine of their care fairly easily. These lizards really are a delight to keep, even if you don't handle them.

I really enjoy watching a chameleon "tuck" itself into bed at night. A few moments before the light turns off ours will return to his favorite nighttime position and curl his tail up for the night.

If you'd like to look into this species, keep in mind Panther Chameleons are lauded for being a little more mild mannered while Veiled Chameleons are known for aggressive tendencies.

## *Common Reptiles*

Snakes are very common reptiles, with corn snake being the most common beginner snake. These snakes don't get very long, don't require special lighting, have a variety of substrate options, and may only need a heating pad to meet their temperature needs. These snakes eat mice.

Anoles are fun, small lizards that are easily found and inexpensive. Their environmental needs are very similar to the crested gecko, but they only feed on insects and require UVB lighting and supplements.

Bearded dragons, making their homes in the desert, are often a reptile keeper's first lizard. However, most people are not informed these lizards need vegetables in their diet as well as insects. Bearded dragons can also get pretty large and need a large enclosure as adults.

Turtles and tortoises are very common in stores, but many can outlive their keepers, and some can get extremely large. Research the type you are considering to ensure it will be a good fit, or if it fits at all. Even a mud turtle, growing to just 5in(13cm) can live for 50 years.

# Niche pets and their sometimes-niche foods

Since reptiles fill so many niches in the wild, their food needs are varied and interesting as well. Here are the most common foods.

## Black soldier fly

You'll find these flies sold as larvae. Some insects like to eat the larvae, but they're also an important option for a pet that wants to catch flying insects. They're high in protein, fat, and calcium. Don't worry, these are not house flies and will not take over your home.

Phoenix worms are a registered trademark variant of black soldier fly larvae.

# _Crickets_

This is one of the most common foods you can offer. Crickets are lively, cheap, and come in an array of sizes most reptiles and amphibians will accept.

On the other hand, the quality of crickets is consistently under scrutiny. They often don't carry a lot of nutrition when they're fed potatoes or dusts and gels that use synthetic proteins. These insects need to be "gut loaded" ahead of time by feeding them nutritious mixes of produce like carrots, squash, and dark, leafy greens.

If you can, keep a larger volume of crickets in their own, designated container. They're much easier to keep alive, on hand, and nutritious. They're cheaper, to boot. I used to pay up to $0.15 a cricket, thinking that was a negligible cost, only to discover my weekly trip could last me easily a month or more had I paid for bulk instead. Buying crickets in bulk, even with shipping, can cut your costs to $0.02 to $0.04 a cricket. At the rate of 200 to 1,000 crickets, that adds up.

Crickets can be stored in a ventilated tub or aquarium with holes too small for a cricket to escape with damp paper towels or water gel and food such as fish flakes or gut loading fruits and veggies like squash. They enjoy having plenty of egg crate to hide in and crawl on.

These common feeders make up the base of many feeding regiments and are high in protein and calcium and low in fat.

Crickets, at their best, are still deficient in minerals like Vitamin A and need to be supplemented.

## Dubia roaches

This option is a little newer in the hobby, despite the gut reaction to having cockroaches in your home. Instead of your average house roach, these are tropical roaches that can't survive the average home's conditions.

These feeders are high in protein and minerals, livelier than superworms and mealworms, and cannot jump, fly or climb. Many keepers are moving over to keeping the dubia roach over crickets.

## Eggs

There are egg-eating snakes! Only one species is known to get large enough to eat small chicken eggs, while most eat quail eggs. If you don't know a guy and your grocery store doesn't offer them, check online reptile stores who can ship them out or a nearby Asian grocery store.

## Fruit flies

Fruit fly cultures you purchase from animal hobbyists aren't your average fruit fly. These species, Drosophila

Hydei and Melanogaster, are special because they are flightless. If you happen to find fruit flies crawling around after a feeding and refusing to fly, then examine your feeding routing and escape options. Otherwise, they won't take over your home.

These feeders are chosen for their incredibly tiny size fit for baby insectivores, dart frogs, and small insects. They are high in protein, low in fat, fairly high in calcium, and very high in phosphorous.

Some sellers of fruit fly cultures also sell kits to split your culture and continue growing fruit flies indefinitely.

If these sound ideal for nearly any pet, keep in mind most pets large enough to eat a cricket or black soldier fly won't consider these worth their time.

## *Fruits and Vegetables*

Some reptiles eat produce!

For fruit-eating reptiles like crested geckos, softer, sweeter, more fragrant fruits like mashed banana, mango, and papaya are usually the preferred.

For reptiles like the bearded dragon, variety is easy. They'll even eat your kale and prunes for you. Most things you can get in your grocery store will work, so just check before you feed it. Here are a few dragon-approved fruits and veggies:

- Apple
- Apricot
- Asparagus
- Bok choy
- Carrot
- Collard greens
- Mustard greens
- Melon, including watermelon
- Okra
- Pear
- Plum
- Pumpkin
- Strawberries
- Turnip greens
- Yellow squash

## Lizards and Anoles

Some reptiles, such as a vine snake, eat anoles. If you're comfortable meeting this need, make sure you have a reliable source for this food.

## Mice

For a reptile, mice are most common for snakes and make up the core of their diet. You can find these frozen in most reptile stores and live at some. Feeding preference varies from snake to snake.

# Nightcrawlers and earthworms

These are just worms, like you find in your garden or for fishing. However, make sure to purchase them from a source that does not treat them with anything rather than getting them from your garden. These worms can carry fertilizers and pesticides from the outside world to your pet and make them sick. Usually, those sold for fishing and those in reptile and aquatic shops understand this importance and are selling healthy, chemical free worms. If you're not sure, just ask.

Store these worms in a moderately cool refrigerator, room temperature is too warm for them.

These feeders are high in protein and calcium.

# Superworms (vs. mealworms)

Superworms and mealworms are used almost interchangeably when discussing this feeder. However, they are different. Mealworms, or Tenebrio molitar, are darkling beetles high in protein and fat. Superworms, or Zophobas morio, is also a darkling beetle closely related to the mealworm, except that these larvae are less chitinous and much easier for your pet to digest.

Nutritionally, these treats are best for variety, protein, and fat. Both superworms and mealworms are common feeders.

ractically, these larvae are known for having a bit of creepy appearance and a tendency to burrow and become a beetle crawling about your enclosures. Of course, they're harmless despite their looks, and the burrowing can be avoided simply by placing them in a feeder dish or hand or tong feeding your pet.

## Supplements

Ensure you are dusting your feeders with a rotation of calcium with D3 and without D3. You will dust at every feeding. When including a multivitamin in your dusting routine, you can simply rotate between the three.

Make sure to ensure the quality of your calcium. This is hugely up to debate, especially as research continues on amphibians and reptiles, but a lot of people swear by RepCal for calcium without D3, while they choose Repashy Calcium Plus for calcium with D3 for amphibians since the retinol in it is more available as a source of Vitamin A for amphibians. On the other hand, reptiles enjoy vitamin mixes with beta carotene as a safer alternative to retinol.

The one option I would certainly shy from is spray on calcium. It's extremely convenient but not reliable or practical. Insects jump away from the sound and wetness, and you can't tell if they're coated. Once you're done, the mixture will calcify your sprayer and stop it from spraying. Save yourself the time and money and stick with powders.

Supplementing, once you know what rotation is best for you and your pet, is very simple to follow.

When purchasing your supplements, if possible, look over reviews for the product. You'll find reputable products will collect a following of experts who even personally test these powders.

When you purchase your supplements and routinely throughout their use, check their dates. These chemicals, even in powder form, do have shelf lives and will not last forever.

## _Waxworms, butterworms_

You'll find these are usually sold in a container to keep them happy for up to a few weeks. You won't want to keep them longer term since these are caterpillars and will morph into large moths. If you happen to lose one in your enclosure, expect to see a large, fluffy moth in the coming weeks that is likely too large for your pet to eat.

These insects, like cheese and ice cream to us, are high in fat and are best reserved as treats or to help a pet put on weight quickly.

# Review of Reptiles

If you've been wavering on getting a reptile because of care, I hope this section covers how easy some can be

nd helps you to look at the needs of the ones you
dmire.

)nce you decide on the type of enclosure you'd like
nd the level of care you're willing to provide, it is very
asy to select a pet from there!

f you are surprised by the cost of set up, you can
heck local postings on sites like craigslist and
ometimes find the exact enclosure or pet or both at a
teep discount. As always with online encounters, err
n the side of safe. If it's not reasonable to meet in a
public space, bring a friend or two or three, just
nclude enough space in the car for your purchase.

# Closing

Pets can be anything from a rock to a hawk in your
ree to a snake native to a region across the world. It's
mpossible to cover all the ins and outs of care for all
he options in this size of a book, but I hope it has
hown you how to think of Animal Welfare for these
opics. In most cases, all it really boils down to is
mimicking their natural habitat and fulfilling their
nutritional needs.

f you're on your way to get a new pet now, I hope you
wo have the best life together!

# About the Expert

**Jessica Child** is an animal lover living in Colorado who cannot help but collect and learn more and more about the Animal Welfare hobby. She has been keeping cats, dogs, and fish since she was a child, and began keeping amphibians and reptiles as an adult. Her newest friends include a St. Bernard / Pyrenees puppy to keep her Labs busy. She has also recently picked up more millipedes and beetles. The beetles are still grubs, munching away every slice of apple offered to them when they're not eating leaves.

In between hunting down extra snacks for these pets, she takes time to find good fried chicken, tacos and salsa, and bread.

HowExpert publishes quick 'how to' guides on unique topics by everyday experts. Visit <u>HowExpert.com</u> to learn more.

# Recommended Resources

www.HowExpert.com – Quick 'How To' Guides on Unique Topics by Everyday Experts.

www.HowExpert.com/writers - Write About Your #1 Passion/Knowledge/Experience.

www.HowExpert.com/membership - Learn a New How To' Topic About Practically Everything Every Week.

www.HowExpert.com/jobs - Check Out HowExpert Jobs.

CPSIA information can be obtained
at www.ICGtesting.com
Printed in the USA
LVHW081423210521
688135LV00002B/205